Questions & Answers
on Love, Sex & Relationships

Love life

A Manual for Singles and Engaged Couples

Volume 1

Dante & Cynthia Veluz
Authors of Hear & Obey and Signs & Wonders
with Nel Ferido-de Guzman

Lovelife

A Manual on Love, Sex & Relationships,
for Singles & Engaged Couples, Volume 1

Unless otherwise stated, all Scripture references are from the New International Version (NIV) of the Bible. Scriptures marked (KJV) are from the King James Version of the Bible.

For any inquiry about the updated **JHMT Calendar of Activities** and for guidelines on how to sponsor a conference or seminar in your area, please visit our website or write, call or visit us at the office address stated below.

Published and distributed by:

JESUS, THE HEART OF MISSIONS TEAM, INC.

An International Network of Christian Leaders & Workers Engaged in Revival & Missions (Affiliated with the Open Bible Faith Fellowship of Canada & Association of International Gospel Assemblies, USA-Phils)

JHMT Network Center • 61 Cambridge Street, Cubao, Quezon City, Metro Manila, Philippines 1109 • **Mailing:** P.O. Box 661, Araneta Center Post Office, Cubao, Quezon City, Metro Manila Philippines 1109 • **Tel. Nos.:** (632) 438-1819 to 21 • **Fax:** (632) 438-1820 • **E-mail:** dantecynthia@hotmail.com or at jhmt@pacific.net.ph • **Website:** www.jhmt.com.ph

Printed in the Republic of the Philippines
By : **CNtoday**
PRINT AND ADS

ISBN: 971-92081-3-9

❦Dedication

*This book is wholeheartedly
dedicated to our heavenly Father,
our Savior and Lord Jesus Christ
and our Lord God Holy Spirit;
to the building up of
the Church, the Body of Christ;
to the singles, engaged and
married couples;
and to the families that have made
Christ the center of their lives.*

❧Acknowledgments

Our special thanks to our very supportive editors and co-workers in God's vineyard, Bro. Bonnie and Zennie Ocampo; to Rev. Jun Cortez for the art works; to Sis. Mhalou Franco, Bro. Neil Acebron, Sis. Reych Haber and Sis. Bituin Acebron for the typesetting and lay-out; to Dr. Milyn Rabara and Dr. Aida Martinez for their proof-reading efforts; to Sis. Esther Penetrante for the lovenotes clippings; to all the other staff of Jesus, the Heart of Missions Team (JHMT); and to all the brethren at Heartbeat of God Global Ministries for their prayers and loving support as we minister to the Body of Christ.

Our loving thanks, too, to our beloved children Eunice, Jonathan and Ruth who have graciously endured the pains of separation from us while we were doing this book; to our parents Bayani & Erling Veluz and Ernie & Belen de Guzman for their usual prayers and support.

🌹Table of Contents

Lovelife

A Manual for Singles & Engaged Couples, Volume 1
Down-to-earth Questions and Answers
on Love Issues for Singles & Engaged Couples

DEDICATION iii
ACKNOWLEDGMENTS iv
TABLE OF CONTENTS v
FOREWORD x
ENDORSEMENTS xiv
PREFACE xviii

INTRODUCTION:
Understanding Love Life Issues
& Family Living xx

CHAPTER 1: LOVE 1
1. What does the Bible say about love? 2
2. When is one ready to fall in love? 4
3. Is it normal to have crushes? Does having a crush
   also mean being in love? What is infatuation? 5
4. Is there such a thing as love at first sight? 9
5. How can you differentiate true love from lust? 10
6. What is the test of true love? 12

CHAPTER 2: SEX 15
1. Is sex evil & sinful? 17
2. What is petting & necking? 18
3. What is the virtue of virginity? 20
4. Is it wrong to masturbate? 21

5. What is wrong with fornication or premarital sex? 23
6. Can pornographic materials be an alternative
    source of sex education? 25
7. What is wrong with homosexuality? 26
8. What are the so-called sexual perversions? 31
9. How do we differentiate sexual diseases? 33

CHAPTER 3:
CHOOSING THE RIGHT PARTNER 35
1. What are the criteria in considering your
    lifetime partner? 35
2. Is the term "considering" the same as courting? 37
3. Can unbelievers be considered? 37
4. How about sharing my faith to the
    unbeliever who courts me?   39
5. How can you be sure that the person you are
    considering is Mr. or Miss Right? 39
6. What if your family opposes your choice
    of a partner? 41
7. Can dreams and impressions serve as guides
    to knowing God's will? 42

CHAPTER 4: BLESSED SINGLENESS 43
1. Why do some people remain single for life? 44
2. How do I overcome the fear of mid-life crisis? 45
3. What activities can singles engage in and excel? 46
4. How should singles be treated in the church? 47
5. How should singles react to pressures? 48
6. Is there still hope for singles? 49
7. How can a single parent cope? 50

CHAPTER 5: COURTSHIP 52
1. Why is the period of courtship critical? 54

2. When is the right time for guys to court
    and for girls to accept suitors? 55
3. How can I overcome fear in courtship? 59
4. Is it proper for women to pursue men? 60
5. What is wrong with matchmaking? 61
6. What is dating? Is it proper to
    date during courtship? 62
7. Can the saying 'May the best man win'
    apply to me and my best friend? 63
8. How can you tell a flirt? 64

CHAPTER 6: ENGAGEMENT 65
1. When are couples considered as engaged? 66
2. How long should an engagement be? 66
3. What preparations are necessary
    during the engagement period? 67
4. What activities can couples engage
    in when they go on dates? 69
5. What are some of the things engaged
    couples need to talk and discuss
    about before marriage? 70
6. Are those into mutual understanding
    (MU) also considered engaged? 72
7. Is counseling a must for engaged
    couples before the wedding? 73
8. What is an engagement vow? 75
9. Should difference in religion stand in
    the way of my engagement? 75
10. What medical tests should engaged couples
    undergo before marriage? 76
11. What is wrong with live-in arrangements? 77
12. How does one cope if his/her partner

breaks the engagement off? 78

13. How would you handle an engagement if you
    found someone else? 79

CHAPTER 7: WEDDING PREPARATIONS 81

1. What are the "first things first" in wedding
   preparations? 83
2. What is *pamanhikan* or *pedida de mano*? 84
3. What is the *despedida de soltera*? 85
4. What is the bridal shower and the stag party? 86
5. What is a dowry? 88
6 What are the ways to have a practical wedding? 89
7. Do you have a checklist for wedding planning? 89
8. What should be the sequence of activities for the
   wedding ceremony and reception program? 99
9. What are the things we need to do
   after the wedding? 105
10. What are the requirements for the application
    of the marriage license? 105
11. If one of the parties is a foreigner, what are the
    requirements for the marriage license?............ 109   12.
What are the formal requisites of marriage
    in the Philippines? 109
13. How does the marriage license and marriage
    contract/certificate differ? 110
14. What is the purpose of the waiting period
    before the marriage license is released? 111
15. Who prepares the marriage contract and
    who submits it? 112
16. What is the use of SECPA and the CTC
    copies of the marriage certificate/contract? 113
17. What happens when the contract/ certificate

of marriage is not submitted on time? ....

18. What are the other requirements if wedding
    ceremony is not held inside the church? 114

19. Is there such a thing as secret marriage(SM)? 115

20. What about tying the knot with a prisoner? 115

21. What is a marriage of exceptional character? 115

22. What about mass weddings? 116

23. Should we have a wedding rehearsal? 117

24. What about additional wedding TIPS? 118

    a. How do we inform our guests that we prefer cash gifts
       instead of presents? 118

    b. Is it proper to enclose bridal registry cards? 118

    c. How important is an R.S.V.P.? 119

    d. What about dress decorum? 119

25. What are some of the common wedding customs? 120

26. What are the other ways to get married? 123

    a. Theme Weddings 124

    b. Weekend Weddings 125

    c. Progressive Weddings 125

    d. Destination Wedding 125

CONCLUSION 128

PRAYER 132

ENDNOTES 133

BIBLIOGRAPHY 136

ABOUT THE AUTHORS 138

🌹 Foreword

Y ou will not only like this book, you will love it because after reading it, you can immediately apply the principles and procedures in your personal, family and ministry life. The concept of the book is not "theology", instead, it is full of principles and lessons that can be confirmed by real-world experiences.

Lovelife is really a manual of timeless teachings that you simply must follow if you want to be successful in your lovelife and family living. The authors, Dante and Cynthia, have boiled down the subject of lovelife from its definition to its final destination, wedding and family life, to a very usable form. As a pastor of a church myself, I have recommended this book to be one of the manuals for Christian Growth teachings to all our pastors and teachers. Not only that, I have talked to other pastors, ministers of the Word and church workers about how this book can help them in their youth and family life ministries, even in organizing their church weddings.

I have always been an avid reader all my life, and I have read somewhere that life, most often times, is just like a merry-go-round. It brings you to where you began. But most everyone agree that we all go around only once in life. We get on board, take a ride around, and exit. The anticipation of the ride is nearly always greater than the actual enjoyment of the ride. If we are honest with ourselves, isn't this also true with most of what we experience in life? But it need not be this way. At the end, we should experience satisfaction and accomplishment, knowing the best is yet to come - looking forward to the "next ride". Why is it so difficult to achieve this feeling of well being? The obvious answer is what happens in between.

This book, as manual, shows the ways and the means that affect our lives, from cradle to grave. Choices are now available to us through this book, they are ours. If we believe them and take them, then it is like the valve that controls the forces shaping the development of our individual characters. We must open the valve all the way to insure ourselves of a constant lifeline to every resource available to us. You may read this book as a manual of true faith, or a transcript that will help you in your self-conquest. But I urge you to read it with an open mind and heart, and a sensitive conscience, for it is a book of love.

REV. BENNY NAVARRO
National Chairman, Association of International
Gospel Assemblies (Philippines - U.S.A.)

🌹 Foreword

Pastors Rodante & Cynthia Veluz have left few stones unturned in this simple question and answer dissertation of hundreds of personal issues that every person must live through. Using the Bible as a basis for sexual and relationship understanding is refreshing.

God made us both sexual and emotional. This is truly a layman's book of knowledge dealing with a frank approach to sex, relationships and spirituality.

Every couple will encounter most, if not all of these issues in their lives. Few of these indivuduals will ever be prompted to discuss or question their feelings and fewer still will have the openness this work provides to them.

They explore the questions that normally hide behind the Holy Grail of professionalism in a straightforward manner. The depth of questioning and the frankness of the approach to the unspoken parts of our lives is outstanding.

Many people have never had the opportunity to approach life from a biblical perspective. This book brings scripture and life together on the same page in a simple but effective manner.

This work is highly recommendable.

REV. ALLEN SKROCH
Senior Pastor, Reaching Out Ministries
Whitehall, Wisconsin, U.S.A.

❧ Foreword

*L*ovelife, by Pastors Dante and Cynthia Veluz, is a must read for every God-fearing man or woman considering marriage. This book deals with important issues that individuals will encounter as they try to please God in their relationships with their "special someone".

I would strongly recommend that parents purchase this book for their children who are reaching maturity and considering God's plan for their lives. It will undoubtedly open new areas for discussions about how to relate to boy friends and girl friends. Their common sense advice on practical issues will help families to work together during this sensitive time.

As a pastor myself, I can see how "Love Life" can be an extremely valuable tool to help couples as they start to develop in their relationship with one another. It will answer many of the questions that they may be too shy to ask others and help open lines of communications between them.

Congratulations to Pastors Dante and Cynthia! You have succeeded in bringing wise counsel to bear on extremely sensitive areas while still being faithful to the Bible's teaching. Your creative use of real questions and answers to common situations brings life to the teaching. Thank you for not shying away from teaching about sex, dating, pornography and AIDS.

REV. RANDY NEILSON
Executive Director, Open Bible
Faith Fellowship of Canada
St. Catharines, Ontario, Canada

🌹 Endorsements

The most often asked questions by this present generation usually pertain to the deep issues of their lives. These should not be taken lightly as mere blabbering of the youth for nothing else to say. Rather, these questions need well-thought of, practical answers given in godly wisdom and in the spirit of understanding and grace. For to whom will our young people turn in their search for direction and meaning, in their time of confusion and doubt but to us, their elders?

Couple authors, Dante and Cynthia Veluz exemplify this type of sensitive, loving eldership in this book, *Lovelife.* They have not only articulated the questions in clear, honest language for our young people today, but their answers are as direct and well-informed as they are biblical. It is a pleasure to have this book in the market.

My young colleagues find the book an enjoyable reading material as the topics raised are along their lines of interest. They find sex issues discussed in sober and truthful manner undergirded by Scriptures. Explanations on certain wedding customs are enlightening making them more appreciative of the wedding rituals.

Lovelife : Volumes 1 & 2 is a must for all church workers and Christian counselors. Every church library should have it, as well as seminaries, high schools and colleges. Let us build our youth rooted in the Faith as they live life to the full under the lordship of our Savior Jesus Christ. Reading good books that provoke thought, help discover the depth of our Christian heritage and gently guide them to a high ethical standard of relationships will be of immense contribution. This book is one of those.

EVELYN MIRANDA-FELICIANO
Author & Trainer-Writer-Lecturer, Institute for Studies
in Asian Church and Culture (ISACC)

🌹 Endorsements

Praise be to God for this wonderful book on love, sex and marriage. Indeed, *Lovelife*, which is authored by the husband and wife team, Dante and Cynthia Veluz, is truly of great source of information and enlightenment, and a sure guide to all the readers, most especially the singles, the engaged and the married couples.

As I went through the pages, I found them very interesting. The question and answer portion reveals the significant facts and delicate concerns, issues on happy and successful marriages.

To all the ministers of the Gospel, lay workers, Christian educators, counselors, and all lovers of wisdom...I highly recommend this manual of instruction, for a well-defined and discussed responsibilities of the future home builders and nation makers - the husband and the wife.

May the anointing and the inspiration of the Holy Spirit be granted upon this book, the readers, and the writers. God bless you all.

REV. DR. ANACLETO LOBARBIO
Radio Host, "Laging Nagmamahal"
District Superintendent, Southern Tagalog District
Council of the Assemblies of God in the Philippines

🌹 Endorsements

*L*ovelife Manual is a handy tool for everybody who is concerned about living right for God.

This manual is very timely and adapted to the Filipino culture. You can find solid answers to the questions people are afraid to ask.

REV. JONATHAN & VICKY SEBASTIAN
Senior Pastor, Jesus Christ Saves Global Outreach

I highly recommend this book to the married couples and those who are planning to get married. It contains practical and biblical answers to the most common problems encountered by couples and singles.

This book will also expedite with ease in the wedding preparations because the concepts and ideas are relevant to the needs of present-day situations.

REV. ARIEL MONEDA
National Chairman, Philippine
Pentecostal Holiness Church

*T*his Lovelife is commendable and worthy for reading by every young person. It is very informative and educational. It explicitly presents biblical foundation and exposition about love, sex and marriage, when the most needed aspects in the lives of teenagers and singles, which their parents seem hesitant or have no time to discuss with them.

BISHOP AMBROCIO PORCINCULA
Moderator, Board of Bishops
Philippine Integrated Mennonite Churches

❦ Endorsements

Certainly, some failures are the result of unavoidable circumstances. But many - perhaps most - are the natural consequences of wrong choices. Many of us choose to get married and some choose to be singles. Even Christians sometimes fail because they seek marriage and love the world's way, according to the world's standard. But on this book you will discover the key in your lovelife tucked away in God's word.

BISHOP LOUIE SALONGA, DMD
Senior Pastor, Jesus the Living Water Church
General Secretary, Quezon City Pastoral Movement

The chapter on "Blessed Singleness" posesses the most common and crucial questions on this much misunderstood, sometimes even maligned state, and answers them clearly and comprehensively from a perspective that spans solidly on our Christian faith. As a single, middle-aged person myself, I firmly believe that God has called me to this vocation and heeding His call, through joy and tears, is what gives meaning to my life in this world.

SIS. CHIT PEÑALOZA
Kamuning Bible Church

Preface

For the last two years of our ministry in the Body of Christ in the Philippines, God has been opening doors for us in the areas of love life and family living. Several times, we have been invited to speak on love, courtship, marriage, and family living. We have been witnesses to couples renewing their marriage vows after genuine repentance and release of forgiveness unto one another. Through God's help and intervention, we saw couples on the verge of divorce, reconciling, after prayer and counseling and eventually acknowledging their need of Jesus Christ as the only hope and answer to their marriage and family problems.

We are also grateful to God for giving us opportunities to minister to singles and engaged couples. God established the fear of the Lord in their hearts that they sought to honor the Lord in their lives and relationships by keeping themselves pure until marriage. They upheld the Word of God and glorified the Lord in the process. As a result, they became blessings to others through their testimonies.

On December 25, 1999, as if to affirm our new ministry, God opened a new door for us through a radio program entitled, *"LOVE LIFE"*, over DZRJ, 810Khz AM Band (Philippines). Barely a month after airing this program, inquiries and requests for counseling and seminars poured in. Some brethren even went out of their way to seek counsel during conferences or after Sunday Worship services. We felt this has now become one of our indispensable ministries for the Body of Christ. Aside from personal counseling, we wanted to further meet the needs of our listeners. The Lord led us to sponsor a special gathering in Metro Manila for our radio program listeners consisting of singles, the engaged and married couples. Encouraged, we continued to conduct several meetings of this nature in other places. Later, the Lord gave us further directions to provide a balanced Christian material about this ministry. Thus, this manual on LOVELIFE.

In these two books, Lovelife Volumes 1 & 2 we have adopted a different format to make it more interesting and adaptable to all ages. In every chapter, we present the biblical teachings on a subject area first then followed by the questions and corresponding answers. Volume 1 is for young people, singles and engaged couples while Volume 2 is for married couples and parents.

Most of the common questions included here were asked during the open forum in our seminars or during our radio or private counseling sessions on love, courtship, sex, marriage, family living and other matters. We purposely withheld the names of those who asked or sent us these questions for confidentiality's sake. We incorporated them in these manuals because we believe these will answer some of the problems and concerns of individuals or couples who may have the same experiences.

We have also included sensitive issues such as the chapter on sex to expound God's perspectives and purpose for it and to give practical guidance to singles and couples contemplating marriage. We pray that you, our readers, will find guidance, enlightenment, direction and godly counsel as you go through each chapter. Most of all, may you experience God and His restoration and find meaning in your relationships as you read along.

Indeed, God proves that He is the Author of life, the Hope and the Answer to every marital and emotional problem.

Dante & Cynthia

🌹Introduction

UNDERSTANDING
LOVELIFE ISSUES

I was surprised one day when I met a lady with a downcast face and troubled spirit. She confessed, "Pastor, the Lord led me to seek counsel from you. Please tell me what to do. My heart is troubled. A young man who is one of my students in a Bible School has sets his eyes on me and I feel drawn to him lately. I have this feeling that he could be the right guy for me, but deep in my heart I am confused and have no peace. Is he God's will for me? Will you inquire from God if I am still getting married?"

In my heart I asked the Lord, "*Lord, is she serious? What shall I do?*" The Lord replied in a still small voice, "*Of course she is serious! She will not come to you all the way for nothing.*" I learned later that she has traveled 12 hours from the province to look for me. Then I asked her, "Sister, I hope you won't mind my asking how old you are." "Fifty-four years old," she replied. "The guy is 25 years old," she added. Hearing this made me realize how serious indeed the problem was!

The Lord gave me a word for her in 2 Corinthians 11:2 which says, "I am jealous for you with a godly jealousy. I promised you to one husband, to Christ, so that I might present you as a pure virgin to him." I told her, "Sister, I believe God wants to let you know that Jesus is your only lifetime partner". "Can I still hope for another?" she pleaded. "Well, let the will of the Lord prevail," I replied. She left with her face still downcast. About five years later we met again. I found out she has remained single and now feels happy. She has finally learned to face reality and conform to the will of the Lord upon her life.

At another time, I heard a sister testify that she prayed, "Lord, give me a husband who hails from anywhere but the *Visayan* Region." Meanwhile a brother also prayed, "Lord, if ever you will give me a wife, she should be anybody but a *Kapampangan* (coming from the *Pampanga* province) because those people talk like birds and are difficult to understand." Several months after, these two, the lady who comes from *Pampanga* and the gentleman from the *Visayan* region were matched by God and were soon married. They now have a baby boy. Both got the opposite of what they prayed for.

We met a married couple who was at the point of breaking their marriage up and have agreed to file a divorce in the United States of America. The issues they raised against each other were disagreement in handling of resources, finances and relationships with in-laws. There was no love left for each other, no sweetness, no transparency. The husband kept complaining about his wife's wrong priorities in life and her unsubmissive attitude. Problems like this can only be solved by divine intervention. After a series of counseling and much prayers, their plan for divorce was aborted. God saved their marriage as each one humbled himself and asked forgiveness from the Lord and from one another. Praise God for the healing and restoration of their marriage.

These are just a few among the so many issues in the area of love life and family living that need to be dealt with in accordance with Christian virtues and biblical principles. This manual is designed to help deal with these problems. We look forward to more changed lives and restored relationships as God uses the pages of this book to minister the fear of the Lord to the ailing hearts in the Christian community and to the nations of the world. This is our earnest prayer.

"Faithfulness
to your loved one
should not be measured
by days, weeks,
months nor years
but by everytime
that you are given
a chance to
prove it."

— Gene Parado

Chapter One

LOVE

Webster's dictionary defines love as "a deep and tender feeling of affection for or attachment or devotion to a person or persons; an expression of one's love or affection; a sexual passion or sexual intercourse; to woo or embrace, kiss, etc. as lovers do". [1]

Evelyn Miranda-Feliciano, a renowned Christian author, wrote about her observations on how people define love: "The world considers love to be a passion that rules a person and must be satisfied by any means. Oftentimes, love is superficially defined as any boy-girl relationship for the reason that it must be love because everyone has a boyfriend or girlfriend. At times, having relationships is to disprove homosexuality or the pressure of being "old maids". It becomes a game of make-believe either for emotional self-affirmation or for social prestige. In this kind of relationship, there may indeed be an honest liking for each other but it is not deep enough to merit the name of sincere and honest love. There is non-deepening relationship, just tentative commitment. No wholehearted sharing, just tokens of thoughtfulness. No deep caring, just superficial concerns. Everything else is just for "show". [2]

True enough. Love is an often misunderstood word among people. Media exposures have fed us with all sorts of artificial, illusory notions about what love is for the opposite sex.[3] Let us take a further look on how people view love according to Gene Parado in his book, *Of Love and Lovers*. He quotes several people's definition of love: Burton, "When poverty comes in at the door, love flies out of the window"; Dorothy Parker, "Love is like quicksilver in the hand. Leave the fingers open, and it stays. Clutch it, and it darts away"; Edwin Arlington Robinson, "Love must have wings to fly away from love, and to fly back again"; and Dr. D. H. Fink, "When love is not demonstrative, it is not love." [4]

As we look at these definitions of love we can observe that each person defines or describes love according to what fits his needs or what his experiences dictate. Very often the definitions are very subjective. In this chapter we are presenting the biblical perspectives that will give us the true meaning and essence of love that is applicable in our lives regardless of our age, sex and religious affiliation.

We gathered the foregoing questions from people who desired to be enlightened on issues about love. We will try to answer them from a spiritual point of view and provide practical suggestions where appropriate.

What does the Bible say about love?

"I want to know why we love different people close to us differently and yet love them in a special way and have different feelings for different relationships."

Ray E. Short, author of *Sex, Love or Infatuation*, shares the five New Testament Greek words for love:[5]

A. *Agape:* Love that is sacrificial, self-giving, committed, undying, just like the love of Christ for His Bride, the Church.

B. *Eros* : Love that refers to romantic love, physical love and desires; drive to unite with something attractive. The English word erotic means passion and sex, but for Greeks, eros could even be used to describe the love for God.

C. *Philia* : Love that is based on friendship and companionship. It is a close feeling that develops when two persons have many

things in common. This is sometimes called brotherly love.

D. *Storge* : Kind of love shared by parents and children or family affection.

E. *Epithymia* : Love that is sensual or sexual desire.

The Bible says that God is love (*agape*, 1 John 4:7). And so great is the Father's love for mankind that He proved it when He gave His only begotten Son, Jesus, to die on the cross to redeem man from eternal damnation (John 3:16). Jesus showed the same love for mankind when He voluntarily offered himself to die on the cross so that through Him we might have life, and have it to the full (John 10:10b). The Apostle Paul further describes the characteristics or true components of *agape* love in 1 Corinthians 13:4-8; 13, as follows:

    a. Patience
    b. Kindness
    c. Not envious
    d. Not boastful

e. Not proud
f. Not rude
g. Not self-seeking
h. Not easily angered
i. Keeps no record of wrongs
j. Does not delight in evil but rejoices with the truth
k. Always protects, trusts, hopes, perseveres
l. Never fails
m. The greatest of what will remain

The characteristics of *agape* love according to Apostle Paul and God's demonstration of love by giving His only begotten Son, Jesus Christ, to die on the cross for the redemption of mankind are to be the basis of our definition of genuine love. Therefore, this means that the one who is in love must be willing to offer his life for the other and reflect genuine character traits stated above.

2 When is one ready to fall in love?

"I am 15 years old and I am falling in love with a classmate who is of the same age. I feel she also likes me a lot. I have started writing short friendly notes to her and I plan to write her a love letter soon. Nowadays, we usually go home together after school. The trouble is, I learned from her brother who is my friend, that when their mom saw my friendly notes, she discerned that my intention is leading to a relationship. She scolded her daughter and warned her that if she finds out that her daughter has a boyfriend she will force her to stop studying. Don't we have the right to love and be loved?"

As a young person, whether you know or admit it or not, your emotions are subjective and volatile. Love requires maturity and readiness which at the moment you lack. At this time, we believe you still have to undergo a lot of preparations before plunging into a relationship. Therefore we advise you not to pursue this relationship at this time and just remain friends with her. Continue to pray for her and pray, too, that you will be able to control your feelings. Refrain from going home together with her and try to divert your attention to other activities. Attend fellowships and involve yourself in church work. In

school, involve yourself in extra-curricular activities like sports, or other wholesome school programs. For as long as you seek God's will for your lives, you will find His best for you. If you are really meant for each other, He will surely preserve both of you until you are altogether ready.

We suggest you develop your relationship with Jesus first. Make Him the Lord of your life. Learn to love Him above all. Once your walk with Jesus is established, you will find fulfillment in Him. Unless you have arrived at this level of maturity when God has become all-sufficient for you, you are not ready to love. When that time comes, He will prepare you to go into a relationship that is truly based on love. In due time He will give you your heart's desire.

Is it normal to have crushes? Does having a crush also mean being in love? What is infatuation?

"I am in high school. This guy in our class is hero to everybody. He is good in academics, in sports, in drama, in school leadership besides

> *being good-looking. I always dream about him.*
> *Sometimes I cannot concentrate in class because*
> *I always stare at him. My friends and I always*
> *talk about him. I always write to him but I*
> *never hand my letters to him, I just keep them*
> *to myself. I do not know if this is still a crush*
> *or I am already falling in love. Can you help*
> *me?"*

For girls and boys like your age or even younger, your feelings are often described as having a "crush" or "infatuation" or what others call as "puppy love". Although there can be strong emotions attached to it, you should not confuse this with love. Love is more than a feeling or a sensation, while infatuation is ruled mostly by feelings. Infatuation is quite normal in early teen's life. This strange stirring within you is brought about by what psychologists and doctors term as secondary sex development or puberty. This has something to do with hormonal body changes and stirrings of new impulses that may cause you confusion and bewilderment, especially because all of a sudden you begin to be physically attracted with the opposite sex. These are tender feelings but they are not enough as bases for love and marriage.

You will notice later that this "feeling" will fade away, and you will eventually see reality. Many times, this feeling is not reciprocated and is a one-way affair, right? For now, the best thing for you to do is to thank God for the fine qualities that He has made in the life of your "crush". It is alright to appreciate someone of the opposite or even of the same sex because of his or her physical features and attributes. It is normal to praise someone because of his assets, his strengths, and his achievements but not to the point of idolizing that person, thinking about him and losing your mind over him. Otherwise, you will only find yourself distracted and unable to fulfill God's plan for your life.

This time is the best time for you to know God and enjoy His very presence, to feel His love and for you to love Him more. It is best for you at this time to concentrate on your studies, and continue to make friends with many young men and women who can be positive influences in your life. Enjoy your teen-age life and do not be obsessed with your crush because one day in the future, God will surely present to you the right guy at the right time. You would not want to miss God's best for you, right?

Here is a test for you to be able to tell the difference between true love and "puppy love". Answer the following questions[6] by yes or no.

1. Do I start to think of the person's feelings and sensitivities rather than my own?
2. Do I bother to find out something else to love in him/her aside from the obvious things and assets he/she has?
3. When I met him/her for the first time, was it really special?
4. Do I take time to know the person?
5. Do I really listen to his/her way of relating his/her needs and try to help?

6. Do I find his/her worst moods tolerable?
7. Am I willing to overlook his/her strange quirks and faults?
8. Do I still remember him/her in the company of someone else?
9. Has this feeling stood the test of compatibility?
10. Can I honestly envision him/her as the future mother or father of my children?
11. Can I risk the possibility of being hurt by him/her?
12. When we quarrel, is my first thought to save the relationship rather than to prove who is right?
13. Can I proudly introduce him/her to my friends and family?
14. Do I take time to be known by him/her?
15. Do I consider (or court) the person along with several others at the same time?
16. Do I find myself constantly comparing him/her with someone else, even with members of my family?
17. Do I give him/her a just cause to be jealous?
18. Do I find myself losing physical control whenever we are alone together, going as far as to initiate petting (outside marriage)?
19. Do I find there is nothing to bind us together other than our intense attraction or physical need for each other?
20. Am I always saying "don't make me wait", and asking proofs of how much he/she loves me?
21. Do I find myself always criticizing or nagging him/her?
22. Do I find it hard to be publicly affectionate to him/her even in some ways?
23. Have I been guilty, as of this moment, of having deceived him/her in some ways?
24. Can I forgive him/her without bearing a grudge?
25. Can I ask for forgiveness readily enough?
26. Has this feeling stood the test of time and separation?

SCORING: From numbers 1-14, the answer should be YES; for numbers 15-23, the answer should be NO; and for number 24-26, YES. Score yourself one point for each correct answer.

0-9 It is puppy love if there ever was one. Try to grow more and let him/her grow more too before saying "I love you". Read 1 Corinthians 13:4-8, repeatedly.

10-18 With a little help from the Author of Love you can shed off most of your illusions and become more realistic, more loving. That is, assuming that both of you do know Jesus, the God of Love, or are striving to know Him (read 1 John 4:7-10).

19-26 Either you have been concentrating on getting the right answers to this quiz, or you are simply growing in love with each other, hardly knowing you've DONE IT! You are an active doer of 1 Corinthians 13, so keep it up, and remember that God should be your FIRST LOVE (1 John5:21).

Is there such a thing as love at first sight?

"I have been rather choosy in my love life. Yet the reason as it seemed to me is that I have not really found the right girl. But you know, something just happened. I suddenly felt different when I met this particular girl in the office for the first time. There was a thud in my heart that I experienced for the first time. I just knew I had to know this girl deeper. Is it possible that I have fallen in love with this girl at first sight?"

In general, many people say there is no such thing as love at first sight because this kind normally springs from superficial attraction. Basically, true love takes time to grow and develop. In your case, it is best if you know yourself and the other person well enough to be certain about it. Go ahead and pursue and explore your feelings. It is right for you to confirm this from the Lord through prayer. Do not be in such a hurry to commit yourself. It would be good also if you can ask advice from mature people for further confirmation. If in the process you find that everything points to a positive direction and you cannot let go of this girl and are willing to live with her for a lifetime, then you probably have found your own true love.

How can you differentiate love from lust?

"I am an overseas worker. My first year outside of the country was the worst in my life. There were times I thought of committing suicide because of extreme loneliness. But the second year became more bearable because of a few friends I met. I met this guy who swept me off my feet. He was such a thoughtful gentleman. We shared many common interests and I always longed for the close of the day so that we could be together. So our relationship deepened. Eventually we moved in together and we were as happy as can be. Then came the bombshell - I learned that my guy has a family back home, and he has lied to me. I felt dejected. I fell sick and could not go on with life. But this guy never left my side. He assured me that he will never leave me and that we can stay that way forever. I could not think of anything else then. All I needed was someone to comfort me. When I recovered, I began to accept things as they were. I could not care less about his family. I only thought about my needs. However, there is this gnawing feeling that I will eventually lose him and I will be alone finally. I suddenly am afraid. I am hopeless yet hopelessly in love as the song says. Please tell me what to do."

You were both victims of loneliness but it does not mean that because you found the cure in each other, you were right for each other. What you are both feeling for each other started as romantic infatuation which was a mixture of emotion and sex and is not genuine love at all. "Those struck by this infatuation become unrealistic and idealistic. This is called pseudo-love or false love".[7]

Love that is true involves commitment which never changes but rather deepens as days go by. True love always seeks the good of the other and does not seek to hurt. It is a selfless desire to do what is best for the other. Anyone who has the fear of God in his life will strive hard to demonstrate his love and make the other happy and fulfilled in life. This kind of love stands the test of time and remains faithful till the end. It does not look at the faults and weaknesses of the partner but rather accepts him or her for what he or she is. One author says, "True love is free from make-believe, from guilt and from fears within and without. It makes people free to be themselves. Free to do good".[8]

True love is free from make-believe, from guilt and from fears within and without.

Your relationship, in the first place, was based on the need for companionship, physical attraction and perhaps sexual passion, held together against your better judgment. It was not based on respect specifically because he lied about his marital status just to be able to make you like him. Couples who truly love each other will naturally end up giving themselves completely to each in marriage, which you cannot do. We agree with you when you said you will eventually lose him because you are not meant for each other. He has a permanent relationship with his family while yours is temporary. Surely he has the responsibility of caring for his family and one day he will be forced to return to them. While you are both there, you are only bound by lust or intense desire to be with each other. You have to face the fact that the longer you stay with him, the less stable and disturbed you will feel because deep in your heart you know yours is a forbidden love affair before God and man.

Moreover, for as long as you are together, you are going against God's purpose of uniting a man and a woman as one flesh through matrimony. By continuing your affair, you are, in fact, destroying the relationship that has been sanctioned by God. God cannot bless you nor can He be with you in that kind of relationship. You are still young. God has someone especially for you if you are willing to surrender to His will and correct your mistake, and if you are willing to wait. Therefore, we strongly advise you to break up with this man. If it is possible for you to transfer to another job and place, do it quickly and make yourself right with God and man. You will find peace for your soul and if you will let God rule your heart, he will forgive you and heal you of the pains. He will enlighten you and will bring you the right guy who will accept your past and will truly love you.

6   What is the test of true love?

> *"My boyfriend wants me to have sex with him to prove my love for him. I disagreed a lot of times. But he was very persistent. He would argue that it's a norm in our society nowadays and that most women he knows say it's alright to have sexual union with their boyfriends for love's sake. This problem in our relationship has become more serious when at one time he challenged me that if I will not give in to his demand it only means that I don't love him and that he will leave me. I still did not give in. I haven't seen him for the past several weeks. What shall I do?"*

True love is never tested by sexual fulfillment through union. If he only asks for sex as a proof of your love, then his love is shallow and lustful. If you give in, you will commit the sin of fornication. Sex is sacred and is God's gift designed only for married couples.

Even if he gets what he wants from you this is not a guarantee that he will marry you or will stay faithful to you. Other cultures may allow sexual union before marriage as a normal practice but as Christians we would rather obey the Lord. Besides, it is not a matter of culture that is important here but our testimony before God.

To be honest with you, most likely, your boyfriend is just 'feeling love' for you. This kind is characterized by strong sexual urges. He is after your body that is why he could not wait until marriage. He needs deliverance from the spirit of lust that causes these strong urges. If he loves you he must be willing to wait until marriage before he touches you. If he doesn't come back to you just because you refused him, be thankful to God because He has spared you from falling into sin and from continuing in a relationship that is not founded on true love.

Below are additional tests that lovers need to pass to ascertain true love. See also the qualities of true love we mentioned in 1 Corinthians 13 and question numbers 3 and 4 above:

a. *Test of Acceptance*: This is a determination to accept the other unconditionally regardless of weaknesses and flaws.

b. *Test of Commitment:* This is the giving of one self wholly to the partner even if the feelings are not there. This is being true and faithful until the end. This means sticking to each other despite odds in life and despite temptations to replace him/her with another.

c. *Test of Time*: This is staying firm, steady and consistent over years of togetherness and absence. This means one does not change mind over time.

d. *Test of Separation*: Distance should increase the love and not diminish it. Absence should make the heart grow fonder for the beloved that he cannot wait for them to be together again.

e. *Test of Sufferings*: Through ups and downs, through pains and sorrows, through trials and sickness, love does not fade.

f. *Test of Respect*: In all ways, a true lover will not seek to defile the beloved. He will always treat her with utmost respect. He will not force himself nor his desires on her but rather wait for the partner until the time is ripe.

Lovelife Specials to the Nations

Chapter One ✤ Love

🌷Chapter Two

SEX

Webster's dictionary defines *sex* as "either of the two divisions, male or female, into which persons, animals, or plants are divided, with reference to their reproductive functions; the character of being male or female; all the attributes by which males and females are distinguished; or anything connected with sexual gratification or reproduction or the urge for these; especially, the attraction of those of one sex for those of the other; sexual intercourse."[1] Generally, the term sex is used to describe the physical union of male and female human beings through sexual intercourse.

The Word of God teaches that sex is a gift from God and that union between a man and woman is exclusively exercised within the context of marriage. Hebrews 13:4 says, "Marriage should be honored by all, and the marriage bed kept pure, for God will judge the adulterer and all the sexually immoral."

This subject on the proper use of sex is a major concern of everyone in society, singles and married couples, young and old. This is primarily because of the fact that a lot of crimes are sex-related and the reason for the break-up of more than 50% of homes has something to do with the wrong use of sex. Even young children in the elementary school level are now very open to discussions about sex and in some places, they are open to the practice of sex. On the other hand, there still remain some who would feel embarrassed, awkward or uncomfortable to discuss sex because they believe it is a very delicate and sensitive issue. Some conservatives even think it is taboo, dirty, and something that we should avoid talking about.

The world view of sex has become distorted mainly because of the wrong and perverse projections in movies, magazines, and dirty talk shows. Sex has become a common topic in casual conversations and green jokes have become widely acceptable, no longer frowned at. Even in recorded music, some composers openly write about sex and these values are often transmitted to the listeners. It is therefore important for us Christians to offer an alternative, the right perspective according to biblical principles, which this chapter would like to address.

God created sex for married couples for three reasons:

a) *For Procreation.* In Genesis 1:28, God said, "Be fruitful and multiply...." God designed human beings to reproduce their kind through the sexual process. Through marriage which is a permanent relationship and commitment, children are born as a blessed gift. God desires humankind to produce godly offspring (Malachi 2:15).

b) *For unity.* This is being one in the flesh. God wanted man to have nobody closer to him than his own wife and vice versa. Nobody should know the spouse more than his/her partner. Malachi 2:15 says, "Has not the Lord made them one? In flesh and spirit they are his." They are no longer two different identities but one.

One flesh here also means being naked to each other or being transparent to one another. They need not hide anything from each other. As Genesis 1: 24-25, "For this reason a man will leave his father and mother and be united to his wife and they will become one flesh. The man and his wife were both naked, and they felt no shame."

c) *For Pleasure.* God intended for the man and his wife to enjoy themselves and have pleasure in this gift. Proverbs 5:18-19 says, "May your fountain be blessed, may you rejoice in the wife of your youth. A loving doe, a graceful deer—may her breasts satisfy you always, may you ever be captivated by her love."

Below are questions from people who seek for the right answers and for enlightenment.

1 Is sex evil and sinful?

"A friend once told me that he doesn't think premarital sex is wrong. He always says that since sex is God's gift, it has to be enjoyed for as long as you do it with the one you love. How should I answer him?"

Sex *per se* is good and sacred, a wonderful gift from God. But it is not for everybody but ONLY for the husband and his wife. It is morally wrong and sinful to engage in sex outside of marriage. This is called the sin of fornication which God condemns (I Thessalonians 4:13, KJV). There are sure consequences to this sin.

Our young people today claim to be living in the so-called times of "New Morality." Many, like your friend, some of them born-again Christians, believe that it is not morally wrong to have sex before marriage. In fact even in many churches, it is not unusual to see already-pregnant brides marching towards their grooms and such have been casually accepted.

A good portion of our youth today, including your friend, has degenerated in his moral standards and succumbed to peer pressure to conform. They are so exposed these days to sex fantasies on television, movies, or the internet that the sacredness of sex has become passè. Our modern society is wanting in biblical understanding. Proper information about sex should be provided at home, in school but most especially in the church. Our youth need to be taught about Christ and His love.

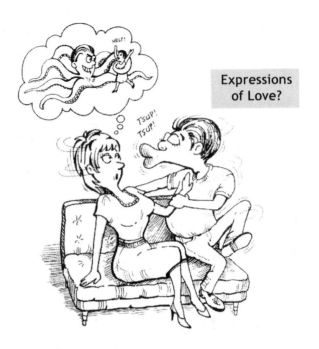

2

What is necking and petting?

> "It is my first time to have a boyfriend. When he first held my hand, I allowed him because I thought it was normal for lovers. After a while, he began to kiss my hand, and little by little his kisses moved up. At first, it was an electrifying experience, but my conscience vehemently said no, although I felt I was beginning to like it. I was afraid that it will result to what others call as necking and petting. What is the difference between the two? Is it normal for sweethearts like us to engage in these?"

Necking is "the act of kissing and caressing in making love"[2] Normally it is done from the neck going up to the face. *Petting*, on the other hand, is "fondling and caressing; involves kissing, embracing, fondling intimately in making love."[3] The area involved here is below the neck going downwards to the sensitive sexual areas of the body.

Caressing and fondling, which are part of the foreplay before intercourse, are only rightfully done within the context of marriage. Therefore it is very dangerous for unmarried couples to engage in these acts. It is nearly

If anyone thinks he is acting improperly toward the virgin he is engaged to, and if she is getting along in years, and he feels he ought to marry, he should do as he wants.

impossible for those who have tasted necking and petting not to go all the way to penetration. When it reaches this point, the lustful desire becomes almost uncontrollable. It is therefore best for you and your boyfriend to refrain from these acts. Ask God's forgiveness and vow not to touch each other again. It is always rewarding to wait until marriage. 1 Corinthians 7:36 says, "If anyone thinks he is acting improperly toward the virgin he is engaged to, and if she is getting along in years, and he feels he ought to marry, he should do as he wants." If you are at the right age and are ready to get married, it would be advisable for you to get married at the soonest possible time. But if you are not, then you have to control yourselves and get rid of lust in your relationship. Honor the Lord and He will guide you into a deeper relationship even without physical contact.

Popular author, Joshua Harris came up with guidelines[4] for people like you to follow in order to avoid sinning against God. As he and his future wife vowed, "We promise each other as long as we are not yet married, that

a) We will not caress each other.
b) We will not "cuddle" each other.
c) We will guard our conversation and meditation, especially regarding intimacy.

d) We will not spend undue amounts of time together
    at late hours."

If all engaged couples are careful to do these things, they will
not only honor each other but will please God. As a result, their
lives will surely be blessed.

3 What is the virtue of virginity?

> "A lot of people say I am quite attrac-
> tive, thus they say it is understandable for
> me to have had three boyfriends. Actually
> that is not quite so. My relationships with
> them were all short-lived. For all three, the
> main reason of our break-up is my being
> conservative, so they claim. Each one of
> them somehow wanted me to go to bed
> with them, but I always stood my ground.
> I want to be different from the rest of my
> generation. I told each one of them that I
> want to reserve my virginity for the one I
> will marry. Although they insisted, it
> became my test for whoever I will marry.
> Do you think there is still such a guy who
> has dignity enough to respect his woman?"

Congratulations for keeping yourself a virgin! You are a rare
gem. What you have done is absolutely right. It is sad that none of
your three boyfriends appreciated you enough to marry you. It
means that none of them truly love you but rather to put it bluntly,
they lust after you. Many young people today fall into deep sin
because they do not resist the desires of the flesh.

God is not only interested in the purity of our soul and spirit,
but He is also concerned with the chastity and purity of our bodies
(1 Thessalonians 5:23). We must realize that our bodies belong to
the Lord and should be used to glorify Him. The Word of God

reminds us that, "The body is not for sexual immorality but for the Lord...therefore glorify God in your body and in your spirit, which are God's" (1 Corinthians 6:13, 20). [Note: *On the other hand, the Lord considers a born-again Christian to be a virgin in spite of his or her past sexual involvements and sin. This is because, "If anyone is in Christ, he is a new creation; the old has gone, the new has come" (2 Corinthians 5:27).*]

My wife Cynthia and I were both virgins when we got married, Even during our college days, we already had the fear of the Lord in our hearts. The Lord preserved us for each other as an answer to our individual prayers. Indeed, our marital relationship for the past 18 years with three children remains strong by His grace because of this principle of honoring the Lord in our lives. We praise God for this testimony that we can share to the world. It is indeed possible for someone to keep himself pure for the life partner that God has preserved for him.

It is an honor and a prize possession when a bride and groom offer themselves virgin to each other. They not only honor each other, but more so honor God. Because of this, they reap the rewards of joy, peace and love that comes from above.

As for you, we suggest that you should not be hasty in getting into a relationship unless you are very sure that the guy is God's choice for you. You need to wait upon the Lord and pray for the right person to come along. You will surely find him. God will surely honor your wanting to remain pure.

Is it wrong to masturbate?

"Ever since I was 12 years old, I have been in the habit of masturbating. When I got born-again, I had a feeling of guilt so I asked a mature Christian if it is wrong. He answered that it is just normal and it is an outlet for active sexual drive. When I was listening to your radio program, I heard you say that it is

Some people would say that masturbation is really having fun and it is a substitute form of gratification when sexual intercourse is impossible. Regardless of other people's defenses or justification, it is still an improper use of sex because it involves sexual fantasies and lustful thoughts that pollute the mind and which are condemned by the Word of God (Colossians 3:5). The term itself, which comes from the Latin word "masturbari" meaning, to pollute one's self, is an indication that it is wrong. It is also known as manustrupation, onanism and self-pollution.[5] It is a common sexual outlet for both boys and girls during their adolescent years which they usually carry with them even during adulthood.

It may be considered by society as normal but it is immoral. It is in fact a sin because it is an act of adultery which Jesus said we commit in our heart when we fantasize or look lustfully a woman (Matthew 5:28). During masturbation, it is quite impossible not to imagine a woman of your fantasy that you are making love with.

Dr. Isabelo Magalit, author of *Why Wait Till Marriage*? writes, "Masturbation is normal only in the sense that masturbation is a widespread practice. However, is it 'normal' to cheat in exams because 'everybody is doing it?' Masturbation is sinful because it is outside God's design for the proper use of sex. It defiles the conscience and must be renounced as sin, even if it is not the worst sin. Like other evil habits, it can only be overcome by the power of the Risen Saviour at work in us by His indwelling Holy Spirit (Romans 8:2)."[6]

Masturbation is sinful because it is outside God's design for the proper use of sex.

What you need to do right now is to come to the Lord Jesus, renounce your sin of lust and ask for deliverance. He can set you free if you desire for it. Jesus has come "...to set the captives free and to release the oppressed" (Luke 4:18-19). Apostle Paul teaches that only Christ can deliver us from any form bondage of the enemy, including lust (Romans 7:21-25). Therefore, make a decision to honor God in your life and consecrate

Only Christ can deliver us from any form of bondage of the enemy.

yourself by asking Him to renew your mind from any impure thought.

What is wrong with fornication or premarital sex?

"I am the leader of the young people's club in our community. I have a problem dealing with two of my members who practice premarital sex and are very vocal about it. Slowly they are influencing the minds of other young people. I have the burden to correct them but I feel inadequate. Can you please teach me what to say?"

You may begin by what the Word of God says, "Now the works of the flesh are evident, which are: adultery, FORNICATION, uncleanness, licentiousness...." (Galatians 5:19, KJV); "For this is the will of God...that you should abstain from FORNICATION..." (1 Thessalonians 4:3, KJV).

The word fornication is mentioned forty-seven times in the New Testament where it is strongly identified as a sexual sin and denounced as a deviation from God's ordained pattern for sexual fulfillment. Defined as sexual intercourse between unmarried individuals of the opposite sex, it usually occurs among those who do not honor the Lord in their lives and could not control themselves because of their bondage to lust. It is also a form of rebellion against the parents and God's commandments.

It comes from a Greek word "PORNEA" where we derive the English term "pornography". In a broader sense, the word fornication includes more than just illicit sexual intercourse. It covers a wide range of sexual sin and perversity such as incest, rape, prostitution, bisexuality, transvestism, sadomasochism, bestiality, exhibitionism and voyeurism. [7]

Righteous leaders like you are what the world needs today. As Christians we need not only teach and counsel, but must pray hard for our young people today that they may have the fear of God. Only God can convict them of wrongdoing. You can start by telling your members about the ill effects of fornication or premarital sex. Sins have sure consequences. If they indulge in this, they will be deprived of enjoyment in their courtship, engagement, wedding and the honeymoon, which are some of the

Encourage your members to confess their sins to God...

most exciting stages of life. Aside from this, fornication may also produce unwanted pregnancy. If the couple involved are students, their future is destroyed, their emotions are ruined, their spiritual lives wrecked and their total person suffers. Oftentimes, the men just want to take advantage of the women and then leave them. Many troubles, including guilt feelings, abortion, and contracting sexual diseases are some of the results of this sin.

Encourage your members to confess their sins to God and turn away from them, and to open up to you. If they are attending church, have them confess to the head minister as well. God is a forgiving God. He can turn their shame into joy. Teach them how to behave toward their boyfriends and girlfriends. Advise them that the safest place for courtship is the home and if ever they would go on dates, it would be good if they will go as a group. This keeps them away from temptations. Meanwhile, they should channel their passion and energy to God. Teach them to love and serve God.

We would like to share with you a list of reasons why premarital sex is wrong. This is based from the book of Ray Short entitled, *Sex, Love or Infatuation*.[8]

a) It tends to break up couples. After their sexual encounter, one or both partners tend to lose interest with one another.

b) A lot of men and women do not want to marry someone who is no longer a virgin. They want to be 'first' as far as the sexual life of their partners are concerned. Many think that those with more sexual experiences are less desirable. Some even brand them as cheap.

c) Couples who have had sexual experiences tend to have less happy marriages.

d) Most often, couples who engage in this, end up in divorce.

e) Those who have experienced premarital sex are likely to have extramarital affairs when they get married. They will find it easier to do this all over again especially with their former partners if ever they meet again.

f) Suspicion between partners creep in. If they have done this to each other, they tend to think that each one can do it again with another person.

g) This experience gets one to marry someone who is not right for him or her. For instance if their union produces pregnancy, the partners are oftentimes forced to marry each other even if they know they are not really meant for each other.

h) Guilt, fears, loss of self-esteem and self-respect result from this wrongdoing.

i) Those who experience sex will be less satisfied with their sex life afterwards.

j) If they do not end up with each other, each of them will tend to compare previous sex experiences. In contrast to the situation where both partners are virgins, there will be no comparisons; their sexual experience becomes pure.

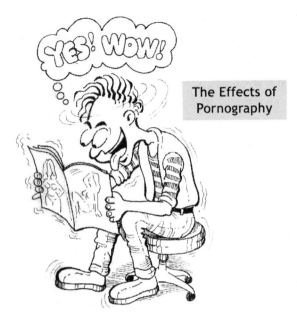

The Effects of
Pornography

k) The partner, especially the woman, will feel she has been used, and will sometimes feel she is just a commodity that can easily be discarded.

Can pornographic materials be an alternate source of sex education?

"My classmate brought his father's Playboy magazine to school one day. At first I felt guilty looking at it but when my classmate laughed at me and insisted that it is for education's sake, I was convinced to read it. I did not quite like some things that I saw and my parents chided me for reading it. Why would adults publish it if it were wrong?"

It seems like your friend has tried to take advantage of your innocence about these things. People peddle perverse materials for money and lust. Some adults have become callous about these things and are no longer considerate about other people's welfare, especially that of the minor's. One day they will be accountable before the Great Judge, our Lord.

Using pornography as a source of sex education is wrong because those materials mostly depict lust and perversion, which is an improper use of sex. Reading these materials is a potentially devastating sin because it is addictive and inevitably leads to deeper sexual experimentation leading to perversion. They will fill your thought life with sensual fantasies and desires. Pornographic lust has been proven to be a major contributing factor to sexual perversion such as rape, incest, prostitution, and child molestation.

The Bible says in the book of Philippians 4:8-9 "...whatever is true, whatever is noble, whatever is right, whatever is pure, whatever is lovely, whatever is admirable - if anything is praiseworthy - think about such things."

7 What is wrong with homosexuality?

"I was a homosexual. I got born-again through a friend who has been so faithful in sharing to me the love of Jesus. I used to evade her a lot of times and even hurled insults at her faith. But in spite of what I was doing she still persisted in sharing the Lord to me. Regardless of my social background I did not feel any form of indifference or discrimination from her. After a year, I surrendered my life to Jesus. However, I still have serious sexual struggles about my past. I feel I am not delivered from it yet. I go to church regularly but I would still feel the same thing with the same sex. My other homosexual friends keep on inviting me to go with them to our usual hang-outs even if I have turned them down so often. They are trying to brainwash me saying that homosexuality is now legitimate and that, once a homo-

> *sexual, always a homosexual'. I am most affected because they tell me my former boyfriend is still waiting and wanting me back. At times, I feel so weak that I feel I might give way to these again. I have given all these things up to the Lord. Please help me, I really want to change."*

The fact that you are admitting your struggles is already an indication that you are sincere in your desire to change. God knows this and it is by this merit, that we believe He will give you much grace to overcome. 1John 5:4 says, "... for everyone born of God overcomes the world. This is the victory that has overcome the world, even our faith." Be sure to fill your thoughts with the word of God. Memorize Scriptures. Renew your mind. Continue to worship God. Do not be idle but rather use your talents for God. Fellowship with believers who are in love with God and have passion for serving Him.

A change of lifestyle as a born-again Christian (or some would call a renewed Christian) is a process, especially for ex-homosexuals like you. You will continue to face temptations but this

Do you not know that the wicked will not inherit the Kingdom of God? Do not be deceived: Neither the sexually immoral, nor homosexual offenders... will inherit the kingdom of God.
- 1 Corinthians 6:9

time the power of God that is in you will enable you to overcome. You need to be faithful and consistent in your walk with God. You have to do all possible measures to renew your ways. Behave as a man and get rid of all feminine ways.

Choose the right company and never compromise your faith again. Avoid going with those friends or better yet if you can avoid

them entirely, do so. Never go to places that you used to hang around in. Resist the offers of your friends with all your might.

Always keep in mind that the Bible speaks strongly against this sin of homosexuality... "Do not lie with a man as one lies with a woman; that is detestable" (Leviticus 18:22); "Do you not know that the wicked will not inherit the kingdom of God? Do not be deceived: Neither the sexually immoral nor idolaters nor adulterers nor male prostitutes nor homosexual offenders..."(1 Corinthians 6:9); "In the same way the men also abandoned natural relations with women and were inflamed with lust for one another. Men committed indecent acts with other men, and received in themselves the due penalty for their perversion" (Romans 1:27).

If you still have anything with you that will remind you of your past, we strongly advise that you burn them. And once you are ready, you can subject yourself to personal deliverance. You may consult a respected Christian counselor, pastor and minister or somebody who is moving in the deliverance ministry.

The problem of homosexuality is brought about by various circumstances. Some homosexuals are in bondage because of a broken home background, especially those who lack parental care or father's image. Some are into it because of transference of spirit through wrong association with friends who are in the same bondage. Some become homosexuals because of rejection from their families that have preference for girls prior to their birth. The homosexual's rejection therefore in this case is a product of frustration. Some boys have been forced into feminine ways because their families encourage them, finding them cute and entertaining. We note therefore that homosexuality is not inborn because God made only two human species, the male and the female.

The so-called "gay movement" especially in the Western society has been very vocal in its attempt to legalize homosexual acts between consenting adults. It has exerted strong influence upon the public consciousness to condone homosexuality as a normal sexual alternative. But in spite of the aggressive attempts to legitimize homosexuality and establish it as an acceptable sexual life-style, the Bible remains unwavering in its strong denunciation of homosexuality as a sexual perversion which is a blatant violation of God's ordained pattern for sexual fulfillment.[9] Homosexuality can never be a normal alternative for anyone.

According to our observations, some homosexual problems are caused by demonic oppression. Therefore these demonic influence need to be broken by the power of God and be cast out. Demons stay in a person's body because they have legal rights to do so. Some demons enter a person's life when his loved ones dedicated him or made an offering for and in his behalf to idols during his conception or early childhood. Some enter the person's life through child molestation or sexual abuse. These things need to be dealt with by divine confrontation. In this case, therefore, the person in bondage needs to submit himself to the deliverance process. Deliverance can come through different ways: through sincere confession to God, through the demonstration of the power of God during counseling or actual deliverance session or through sheer determination to keep oneself away from temptation and sin. *[Some of the teachings on the deliverance ministry can be found on our book on "Signs & Wonders" (Vol. 2, Apostolic Ministry, published by Jesus the Heart of Missions Teams, October, 1999)].*

Note: *There are also Christian organizations which minister specifically to those struggling with sexual and relational problems. One such ministry is the Desert Stream Ministries which provides Christ-centered help for people struggling with sexual and relational problems. You can reach them at www.desertstream.org. In the Philippines, it works closely with Wholeness Ministries. You can reach their national coordinator through virmi@uplink.com.ph.*

8 What are those so-called sexual perversions?

> *"I used to go with a company of sexual perverts. We had orgies together for nights as we smoked pot. But thanks be to God, He saved me and now I have the burden and really want to be used by God to teach young people like me to avoid these grievous sins. Please give me pointers on how to share about these things."*

We thank God that you are now free from this bondage. We are happy that you have chosen us to help you in your crusade against perversions. Your testimony by itself is a very powerful tool. You can share with young people how God delivered you from this lust of the flesh. Then if they are open to the Gospel, share about the love and forgiveness of Jesus that caused you to change.

Some of the practical tips you can advise are avoiding corrupt company and burning of materials such as pornographic magazines, tabloids, posters, websites and movies which are associated with this sin. If their struggles still persist, advise them to seek outside help from spiritual counselors, Christian medical doctors and sex therapists for deliverance. JHMT, through its medical arm, the Jesus, the Healer Medical Missions Team Foundation offers this kind of service.

There are different kinds of sexual perversions[10] or the improper use of sex which are contrary to the Scriptures and God's laws.

a) *Orgies* refers to group sex, having sexual union with one partner to another, either of the same or opposite sex;

b) *Homosexuality* is sexual activity, sexual attraction towards or sexual behavior involving individuals of the same sex;

c) *Incest* is sexual relations with any close relative;

d) *Prostitution* is sexual activity in exchange for money as a means of living;

e) *Rape* is the crime of having sexual intercourse with a woman or a man (like Joseph, Genesis 39:6-23) forcibly and without her/his consent;

f) **Child molestation** refers to sexual relations with a child or a minor;

g) *Bisexuality* is the presence of the qualities of both sexes in the same individual who is attracted to members of both sexes;

h) *Transvestism* is sexual variation in which pleasure is derived from wearing clothes of the opposite sex;

i) *Transsexualism* is conversion from one gender to another, generally by surgery, "sex change," and is often used to describe the desire to change sex organ;

j) *Sadism* is sexual variation in which pleasure is derived from inflicting pain of humiliation on a lover. It gets pleasure from dominating, mistreating, hurting one's partner, physically or otherwise;

k) *Sodomy* is a legal term for the act of anal sex between men, or a man and a woman;

l) *Bestiality* is sexual relations with an animal which normally occurs in rural areas;

m) *Exhibitionism* is the act of publicly exposing one's body usually the genitals or the actual sexual intercourse for the pleasure of the audience and for a fee;

n) *Voyeurism* is peeping at somebody which involves sexual fantasy;

o) *Nymphomania* is an uncontrollable and excessive sexual desire in man or woman (Leviticus 18:1-24; Romans 1:26-27; Galatians 5:19-21);

p) *Masochism* is the getting of sexual pleasure from being dominated, mistreated, or hurt physically or otherwise by one's partner.

All the above-stated sexual perversions fall under sexual immorality. The Bible speaks about the body not being meant for sexual immorality (1 Corinthians 6:13). It says that the body is for the Lord and Lord for the body. Verse 16 says, "Do you not know that he who unites himself with a prostitute is one with her in body?" Verses 18-20 further says, "Flee from sexual immorality." All other sins a man commits are outside his body, but he who sins sexually sins against his own body. Do you know that your body is a temple of the Holy Spirit, who is in you?" The Bible also warns us in 1 Corinthians 6:9-10, "Do you not know that the wicked will not inherit the kingdom of God? Do not be deceived. Neither the sexually immoral nor idolaters nor adulterous nor male prostitutes nor homosexual offenders will inherit the kingdom of God."

How do we differentiate sexual diseases?

"I am suffering from severe pain in my genitals. My friend advised me to consult a doctor for possible gonorrhea. I suppose it is too late for me to undo what I did, for this was a sure consequence of my past sexual relationships with various women, particularly with prostitutes. How will I know if what I have is AIDS? I am afraid and I feel embarrassed. I don't know what to do, please help me."

Venereal diseases are caused by highly specific infections almost always acquired during sexual act. Bacteria or fungi that cause venereal diseases can generally attack certain portions of the body including the genital tract. A more serious sexually transmitted disease is AIDS which is considered by some as incurable, though some medical findings say that the life duration of the patient can now be prolonged. Listed below are some common sexual diseases[11].

a) *AIDS (Acquired Immune Deficiency Syndrome)* is the last stage of an infection caused by HIV (Human Immune Deficiency Virus) which is the virus that destroys the immune system, leaving the person increasingly defenseless against all infections and some cancers. From the time a person is infected with HIV, AIDS takes 10 years to develop. Most, if not all HIV positive people will develop AIDS. HIV-infected people who do not have AIDS will spread the virus since they usually live for many years without exhibiting any sign of the disease and may be passing it to others. Medical studies show that HIV is transmitted through any of the following: sexual intercourse, transfusion of HIV contaminated blood, sharing of needles (especially among drug abusers), ear piercing or tattooing with unclean needles, or a woman can pass the virus to her baby during pregnancy, during birth or shortly after birth or through breastfeeding;

b) *Gonorrhea* is a venereal disease caused by gonococci, characterized by inflammation of the mucous membrane of the genitorary tract with a discharge of mucous and pus, usually transmitted by sexual intercourse;

c) *Syphilis* is a contagious venereal disease. It is caused by a spirochete (spiral-shaped bacterium, *Treponema pallidum*). The germ is usually transmitted by sexual contact. It is one of the most dangerous of the sexual diseases, next to AIDS.

Only proper medical laboratory examinations will show what kind of sexual disease you have acquired. We strongly advise you to consult a doctor for this purpose and apply proper medical treatment the soonest time possible. At this time, you need to ask God to forgive you and help you be delivered from such wrong doing. Our God is a healing God and He will not drive away those who humble themselves before Him. He is able to heal even the hopeless kind of sexual disease. Finally, the only way to avoid any form of sexual disease is never to engaged in any of the sexual sins as mentioned above. Seek to honor the Lord in your life.

Chapter Three

CHOOSING THE RIGHT PARTNER

T he word of God says, "A man's steps are directed by the Lord" (Proverbs 16:9). Moreover, it is written, "He who finds a wife finds what is good and receives favor from the Lord" (Proverbs 18:22).

In Genesis 2, we find that it is the Lord God who brought the woman to the man. It is God who created and chose the right person suitable for the man. And His choice is always perfect. It is therefore, ideal and beneficial that if a man or a woman would take a partner, he or she should allow God to direct his steps and have His way in his/her life. This is the key to having a good married life and having favor from the Lord. May God use this chapter to guide you in the right choice of a mate.

What are the criteria in considering your lifetime partner?

"I am the kind of person who acts only when my steps are sure. This is the reason why I reached this age without a partner. I often consult my friends to ask what they feel about my moves. This time, I am keeping it to myself because I do not want to be embarrassed or humiliated. I believe I am falling in love but I really want to be sure that I will not make a mistake in taking her as my partner. Maybe you can help me."

You really have to consider a lot of things before committing yourself to a mate. Here is a list of guidelines that we hope can help you in choosing your life partner.

a) **Check yourself** – your motive. Is the cause of attraction purely physical? Some guys woo a girl just to have somebody to display to friends.

b) **As you pray, wait upon God.** But remember that waiting doesn't mean you won't do anything. He may reveal His will through the Scriptures, through visions, dreams, etc. When it is God who reveals and you obey, you will never go wrong. I prayed for 6 months for my wife Cynthia without sharing it to anyone. We know of a guy who prayed for 14 months before courtship. God has blessed our relationships.

c) **Be prepared** emotionally, financially, socially, mentally and spiritually (Romans 12:1). Be sure that you keep yourself pure and free from lust (Hebrews 13:4; Matthew 5:28).

d) **Likewise, observe** if the girl matches your spiritual fervor and emotional maturity. She may not be financially ready, nor socially mature, but these are of lesser importance than the first two.

e) **Ask for counsel and confirmation** from others, especially your parents and family, pastors, godly friends. If there is a witness in their spirit, most likely you are on the right track.

f) **Get to know each other.** Know his/her likes and dislikes, ambition & calling, family background, physical/health condition, sports, hobbies, friends. Find out if your personalities complement each other.

g) **Visit her home** so you can get acquainted with her family and relatives. Observe their lifestyles. By these you will know if she is a potential lifetime partner.

h) **If you are definitely sure of her**, and you feel that you can live with her, with all her strengths and weaknesses, then you can start courting and later enter into a commitment .

i) **Ask for the consent** of the other party for prayer consideration. She has to have the same witness in her spirit. The feeling must be mutual, too.

2 Is the term 'considering' the same as courting?

> "*Someone in church approached me and admitted to me that he is considering and praying for me. Does this mean that he has started courting me? Can we go out together at this stage of consideration?*"

The term considering is different from courting. The former is an expressed intention to carefully pray and study if one is the will of God for the other. There is no courtship involved at this stage. This is the time that the guy who approached you seeks God and finds out if you are God's will for him. In turn, he also expects you to do the same.

Once he has made sure of God's will, then it will be the time he will formally court you. At this stage of consideration, however, it is best if you do not go out together by yourselves. It will be worthwhile to learn each other's likes and dislikes and get to know each other while amongst the other brethren or in the company of friends.

3 Can unbelievers be considered?

> "*I have been a born-again Christian for two years. I have always read and heard that I am not supposed to entertain unbelievers. I had a boyfriend before I came to know the Lord but in obedience to Him, I gave him up. But after that, I never had any Christian suitor. Right now there is this guy who I believe is any girl's dream: looks, attitude, money, everything else except his faith. I think I am falling for him. He is more kind and thoughtful than any Christian man I*

know. He loves me so much and is so persistent and would not take no for an answer. What shall I do?"

This is a matter of knowing who weighs more to you. This also calls for undivided obedience to God. The Lord commands in 2 Corinthians 6:14 that we should "not be yoked with unbelievers. For what do righteousness and wickedness have in common? Or what fellowship can light have with darkness?" The instruction is simple. God does not allow it and that there is no exception. God cannot be wrong in giving us this command. He knows and can foresee that marrying an unbeliever will bring us heartaches and pains in the future and will only draw us away from Him.

I know of a woman believer who married a very kind-hearted guy but who does not have a personal relationship with Jesus. According to her, he is almost a perfect husband and father, except that it pains her that every Sunday they would go separate ways. She attends the fellowship while her husband and children go to another church. She could not share the joys she has, nor can she freely accept and entertain the brethren in her home for fear of her husband. She could not pray aloud when her children get sick. She cannot worship God freely inside her home. She and her husband have totally different views about values in life. In short, she is not happy. She often goes back to God for forgiveness for her disobedience. These may seem like minor differences and yet can cause a lot of problems.

How about sharing my faith to the unbeliever who courts me?

"The guy who is courting me is not a Christian but I love and want to marry him. I know that in the process of courtship as I share my faith, he will come to know the Lord. Do you confirm this?"

It is very dangerous to entertain unbelieving suitors. You see, the law of gravity illustrates that it is easier to pull a person down into the pit than for someone to pull him up.

Sharing the Christian faith must be done without ulterior motives. Most likely the guy will agree to accept your faith just to win your favor but without genuine conversion. But if you really want him to be saved, let someone else share the gospel to him. As for you, consider what the Bible says about obedience to God. If you really love God, then you have to obey what His Word says. Most of those we know who entertained unbelieving suitors fell into the trap of the enemy and suffered the consequences because of their disobedience to God. Some ended up as battered wives while others suffered from broken marriages. Many of them lost their first love for God.

How can you be sure that the person you are considering is Mr. or Miss Right?

"I am a professional and for so long I have waited for my lifetime partner. Now I have the opportu-

nity to choose between two suitors. One is my officemate—tall, good-looking, a professional like me and the other is a townmate who visited Manila and stayed in our house for a week. He is okay, although not as handsome. The trouble with the first suitor is that I heard that he has had a lot of girlfriends, although he promised that I will be his last because he has found Miss Right in me. Besides, he has a very active night life. But I believe that I can change his negative character. My townmate, on the other hand, is very thoughtful and serious with me. I noticed that he is so much at peace with himself and the world. He is not aggressive but every inch a gentlemen. He does not seem to be ambitious and his tastes are simple and has no vices. Although they are both attractive to me, I seem to be more inclined to the first. Please advise me which of the two should I choose.

Ideal Mate?

You are very blessed to have two suitors when others do not even have one. Anyway, the choice you will make means a lifetime commitment. Therefore, you really have to be sure of your choice. Good looks, physical attraction and bare promises will never guarantee your happiness in life. As you well know, beauty fades but strength in character is a treasure forever. Be sure to pray hard for this decision.

Aside from the pointers we gave you, below are some questions that you can consider before you make a decision:

a) Is the man ready to say that he is willing to marry you? If he is serious with God and is a responsible person, then he is worthy to be considered.

b) Does he want to be known and does he want to know you more? Try to observe him in different situations. Do you know anything about his background? If possible, you must see the best and worst of him in church, at home, during his work time or play time, with his relatives and even with friends for you to know if you can accept not only his strengths but also his weaknesses.

c) Is he respectful and patient to wait upon God and upon your decision?

d) Has he passed the approval of people who love you and are concerned with you? Opinions of concerned people will help shed light.

What if your family opposes your choice of a partner?

"My best friend who is 28 years old, is considering a brother in church and after praying for sometime, she is sure that he is God's will for her. She consulted our pastor and elders and they also approved of her choice. The problem is that although her father and brothers approves of her choice, her mother strongly disapproves because the guy looks much older than she is."

It is true that sons and daughters should seek confirmation about the love of their life from their parents and family. Most often than not, especially for those who are quite young, the counsel of parents are very valuable and they have been given wisdom by God to know what is best for their children. Thus, children should obey them even in this area. There are cases, however, when parents can be overprotective to the point of being selfish that they can no longer discern what God's will for their child.

In the case of your friend it is very possible that the mother is just biased against the guy. But because your friend has waited for God's will in her life and has asked a lot of confirmations from God and from other people who can help her in her decision, she can decide without her mother's consent. But she should make her mother understand why she is going against her wishes. Later on, once the two have established their relationship, advise your friend to make her boyfriend win the favor of his future mother-in-law. He should prove to her mother that her daughter did not make a mistake in her choice.

 ### Can dreams and impression serve as guides in knowing God's will?

"I had this exciting dream about a woman whom I am to wed. I know I have not met this girl before but when I woke up, I felt in my spirit that she is the one for me. Now I have this desire to find this woman. Is it possible that God has already revealed my future wife through my dreams and impressions?"

God does sometimes speak through dreams and impressions. There are dreams however which are products of too much thinking or desire. In your case, it could be a prophetic dream. Let us just give you a warning that you do not get obsessed with that woman in your dream and be distracted in doing what God wants you to accomplish. Wait upon the Lord but prepare yourself for God's will. Open your eyes and heart but remember to keep yourself pure.

🌿Chapter Four

BLESSED SINGLENESS

This chapter deals on the facts of life regarding singlehood. While it is true that God said in Genesis 2:18, "that it is not good for a man to be alone", the Bible also discusses the reasons why some remain unmarried. How should singles then cope with life's realities? We urge you to read on.

Why do some people remain single for life?

"Up to now I am still wondering why my aunt who is so pretty and intelligent did not get married. I heard that she has had suitors when she was younger. Why are there people like her who seem 'called' to be singles for life?"

We can find the answers from the Bible itself. Your aunt may have remained single because of any of the three reasons mentioned here below. In Matthew 19:10-12, when the disciples told Jesus that if marriage brings so much complications, it is better not to marry. Jesus gave four reasons why some remain single throughout their lives:

a) *It is a gift.* Verse 11 says, "not everyone can accept the word" that they ought not to marry, "but only those to whom it has been given". There is this so-called gift of celibacy. Since it is a gift, it must be good. Those who receive this gift accept it with great joy. They are fulfilled and contented in their status. They are not bothered by attraction with the opposite sex nor by sexual urges. God made them so! We know of an English missionary, still good looking at 70, whom you will never find sulking, lonely or downcast. He is one person who is radiantly happy and contented with his life.

b) Another reason why some remain single throughout their lives is because *they are eunuchs* (verse 12) and they were born that way. We do not have eunuchs among us, because they were Jews in Jesus' time who served at the temple and they castrated (removed their sex organs) themselves so that they would not be tempted to marry and have children.

c) The third reason why some remain single is *because they were made that way by men* (verse 12). I know of three daughters in a family who grew old who did not get married because their parents were so strict. The parents would watch over their every move. When one of them was already working, the parents would guard her and bring her to and from her workplace.

Another example is a movie actress who was gang-raped. After 30 years, she is still a man-hater. They were all made that way by men.

d) Verse 12 says, others have renounced marriage because of the kingdom of heaven. These are men and women who by their choice gave up their rights to marry in order to devote their lives to God. Born again pastors, church workers and Roman Catholic priests and nuns who want to concentrate on the work of God find it a joy to serve Him alone.

An American prophet by the name of Paul Cain used to have a sweetheart whom the Lord asked him to give up. He asked the Lord to take away the love and affection that each one has for the other. And the Lord did. Without any hesitation, he gave her up and thereafter became a celibate all his life. He is happily serving God until now.

2   How do I overcome the fear of mid-life crisis?

"I am 39 years old, still single though not by choice. I think I am going through one of the most difficult times in my life. I am going through a crisis and am losing hope and the joy of living. I feel I am up to no good, that my life is one long monotony and routine. As I am single, nothing seems to drive me or motivate me further. I always envy my batchmates who now have children of their own with loving husbands who take care of them. Me, I feel so alone. What shall I do?"

Do not despair. The book of Isaiah says that God is your husband. He is far more caring, loving, sweeter than any husband could be. With Him you can be fully whole, fulfilled and contented. If you will get to know Him and pour out your life in obedience to what He says in His word for you, you will need no one else. You will find security and joy being in His presence. How do you do this?

Spend more time in knowing God by reading His word, the Bible. Pray, pour out your soul and tell Him everything you feel inside without reservations, like a friend or a lover would. Worship Him with all your heart, singing songs of love, worship and praise. Look for people who love God as much and fellowship with them. Reach out to other people. Open your eyes and you will find that there are a lot of people who need you and to whom you can extend the love of God. There is nothing more rewarding and more satisfying than these. Try these solutions.

3 What activities can singles engage in and excel?

"I feel so bored and depressed about my life at 40. I could not think of anything to do to make me forget the pain my former boyfriend inflicted upon me when he married somebody else. Life seems to drag on. What should I do now?"

There is no use living in the past. Spring back to life. Look to the fields, appreciate the sunshine. Observe the happy children laughing. Listen to the birds. It is great to be alive! Always look at the future, be optimistic because it is God who holds the future. The psalmist says, "Why so downcast o my soul, put your hope in God."

At the Jesus the Heart of Missions Team office in Cubao, we have single ladies and men, ranging from 45 down to 23 years old, whose minds do not dwell on who they will marry or whether they will have suitors. Their minds are preoccupied with the things of God. They love God and serve Him with all their hearts and they trust Him to provide every need, even life partners if He wills.

Some are involved in medical missions even if not all of them are medical practitioners. Others are involved in mercy ministries. They regularly feed the street children, treat them out, buy them clothes. They also mobilize people to help these less fortunate ones. They are involved in visiting and praying for the prisoners. They conduct camps for children and for singles like you. They are in-

But in all these things, remember that only in God can you find the fulness of joy. If you are intimate with God, you will lack nothing.

volved in creative arts, mime, drama, and dances for the Lord. They teach other people the Word of God. Whenever the Lord permits, they go to tribal missions in the Philippines and even in foreign lands. THEY HAVE THEIR HANDS FULL. You will never find them sulking nor idle. You can get in touch with these people and fellowship with them. They are contagious in their love for God! (*See the JHMT address and phone numbers at the back of the inside page cover.*)

Perhaps you can also look for friends or acquaintances who are fulfilled singles. Ask them to give you counsel and let them pray over you. Find out what gives them pleasure. Observe their lives and follow their footsteps. Be inspired by them. But in all these things, remember that only in God can you find the fullness of joy. If you are intimate with God, you will lack nothing.

4 How should singles be treated in church?

"Do you have suggestions on how to treat the singles in our church? It seems that they are becoming more of a burden these days because of misbehaviors. Some are in a way running after our single men. As a result, men evade them. Some people make fun of their situation and thereby cause strains in the relationship. Please help."

First things first. You should meet them and confront them about the issue. They should be given exhortations on how women should behave towards the opposite sex and learn modesty. If only every single person would have the right perspective about love and the love of Jesus, they really would be content in whatever state they are in. Therefore, each one should be encouraged to be soaked in the Word of God, and to get closer to God.

As a whole, they should be given projects that they can excel in. In one church I know, they were involved in livelihood programs during their spare time. They made and decorated candles and sold them. This activity was a corporate fund raising for the church kids camp. Now their products are so in demand they have no time left to do unworthy things. In another church, the pastor assigned them to take care of the older folks, training the latter as members of a choir. Now this choir, together with the singles, gets invited by other churches and during social functions because they are excellent singers.

5 How should singles react to pressures?

"I don't like people teasing me because I'm still single at 31. People ask, how come you are not married yet? They senselessly compare me with most of my colleagues who are either engaged or already married. My brother even suggested that I get married to just anybody around so I would not be restless. But the problem is nobody seems interested to court me. I thought I could handle the situation. But really I'm becoming bitter in my heart towards them. Please help me."

Some people can be cruel without them knowing it. We understand the hurts they are causing you but you have to release your forgiveness. You do not have to dwell in self-pity. Prove to them that even if you do not have a boyfriend, you can still be happy and fulfilled as long as Jesus is the center of your life. Remind them that although you are single, you are satisfied. Involve yourself in worthwhile church activities and programs. Be part of the worship team, evangelism team, children's ministry or the ministry of help team. You can even organize a group yourself, such as calamity or emergency team that will respond to disasters or be part of a group that distributes relief to the poor.

Fellowship with other believers and keep yourself busy. Use your creativity and engage in things that can be used for God's glory such as painting, writing songs or plays and other hobbies. Be productive. Depression sets in with idleness.

6 Is there still hope for singles?

> *"I'm 54 years old and still hoping that the Lord will give me a lifetime partner. I know the Lord will grant my desire. I'm holding on to the promises of God for my life. I never give up on this hope. Do you agree with me?"*

If you will go back to our introduction, we cited a similar situation. In the case of that sister, the word of the Lord was for her to remain single. When she accepted that word, she became a better person. In your case, we say, only God knows if He still has somebody for you to share your life with. But for the meantime, you should not pin your hopes on it. Whether or not He gives you a partner, you can still live a full life. You should not be hindered in whatever God planned for you even as a single. If He does give you a partner then He has a purpose for it. In either case you should always praise God.

This is not saying, however, that those who are forty or above will no longer get married. On the contrary, I have a friend who was 41 years old when she got married to a man whom God preserved for her. The man was 60 years old then and never had a girlfriend before her. We wrote her account in our first book, Hear & Obey, Chapter 12, "How to Respond To and Fulfill Personal Prophecy", p. 187.

"My (Cynthia) former officemate, who is a now a full time church worker, was prophesied over several times by foreign prophets. They de-

clared that although she was already nearing her 40's, she did not have the call of celibacy, and that she would resign from full-time ministry and marry a foreigner. Several years went by and it seemed, to many impatient witnesses, that the word would never come to pass. Some people close to her even got frustrated out of concern for her, but she treasured the words of God in her heart.

Sometime in September 1994, this sister called and informed me that the prophecy was nearing fulfillment. Her fiance, a foreigner, would be marrying her by the following year. In October 1995, she got married to this man. Dante and I graced this joyous occasion. She was so delighted that God granted the desire of her heart."

We also know of a lady who is a leader of the Navigators' group who got married at age 52 and still begot one child. God is the giver of every good and perfect gift. Were you asking about hope?

7 How can a single parent cope?

"I am an unwed mother. I have lived through shame, guilt and regret for the wrong things I have done that brought forth my illegitimate child. Now that my daughter is growing and is asking many questions about her father and demanding for many things, I am beginning to feel the shame and guilt all over again. I want to give her more but I am limited as far as resources are concerned. Once I was tempted to give in to the request of a D.O.M. (dirty old man) just to be able to supply my child's wishes for good things. What shall I do?"

If you have confessed and repented of your sins, remember that Jesus does not condemn you. He also takes away your guilt. When your child is old enough to understand, tell her the truth. Assure her of God's forgiveness and love in spite of what happened. Pray that God will give her a heart that understands. Then ask God for grace to give you strength each day to be able to fulfill both the role of a mother and father to your child.

With God's help and with your perseverance, you will be able to raise your child up. But never fall into the temptation of committing another sin. In Isaiah 52, "But your iniquity has made a separation between you and your God, so that He does not hear." Can you bear to be separated from your God? Will you stand to lose your integrity once more?

One last piece of advice- you should not give in to your child's every wish. Give her what she needs but do not spoil her. She does not have to live in luxury even if you can afford it. God bless you as you put your trust completely in Him.

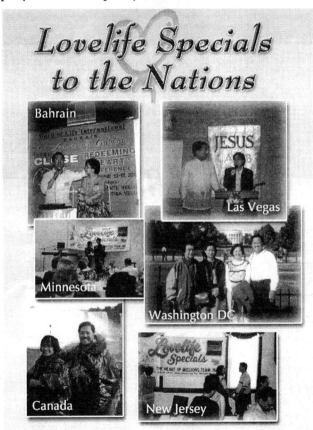

"With all thy faults,
I love thee still."

　　　　　　- William Cowper

🌷Chapter Five

COURTSHIP

Courtship, by Webster's definition is "the act, process, or a period of courting, or wooing".[1] This means that courtship is a time for knowing and winning each other for a permanent commitment. This is a time when a man is almost certain about the lady he has chosen to be his lifetime partner, so that he is ready to say that he is willing to marry her. It is also an opportune time for a man and a woman to know and appreciate each other better.

The Bible gives us an example of courtship worthy of emulation: that of Jacob for Rachel. It took Jacob seven years of service to Laban, his would-be father in law, to prove his love for Rachel. But those seven years seemed like only a few days because of his love for her (Genesis 29:18-20). We see here that a person in love truly knows no bounds. Jacob was willing to sacrifice and wait. May lovers learn the virtue of patience.

This courtship is similar to the old practice among Filipinos especially in the rural areas wherein men have to woo the family of the girl by fetching water, cutting wood and doing all kinds of services. Needless to say that the ways of courtship have evolved to the point that now, some men no longer go through courtship but rather just plunge into a relationship through mutual understanding with the women. The discussions below, we hope, will give you a better understanding on why courtship is important.

Why is the period of courtship critical?

"I am so frustrated with my fiancé. We met three weeks ago and since we both felt it was love at first sight, we decided we would get married as soon as possible. Now I am having second thoughts because we seem to be disagreeing in many ways and it seems to me as our wedding approaches, the more I feel we are not compatible. I am just learning about his idiosyncrasies and irresponsibility. Can I still get out of this mess?"

As we analyzed your problem, we concluded that what was lacking in your relationship is the courtship period. We believe that your problem is a consequence of not having known the true character of your man during courtship. You could have probably saved yourself a lot of trouble if you had gone through a courtship period.

You see, courtship is a time of getting to know the potential of a person as your lifetime partner. This is a time when each one

should exert efforts to know the would-be partner's past and present life as well as his/her future plans. This is a good time to know the person's educational and family background, his/her values, likes and dislikes, working and eating habits, the recreation and sports he/she loves, the nature of his/her job or church ministry involvement, company of friends, health condition and the like. This is the time to discover his/her personality and his/her spiritual maturity. When sufficient information is gathered, then that is the proper time one can make a sound decision whether he can live with that person the rest of his life.

The period of courtship therefore should never be taken for granted. What you discover about each other during courtship will have a great bearing on the success or failure of your marriage later. If at this stage you observe flaws in the person you are courting and think that you can overlook them for the moment and you can later change your partner, you are in for a disappointment. You will never be able to change his character. You can only trust God to do that. You might as well find out now if you can live with this person's flaws all your life.

As for you, we suggest that you pray hard for this decision. It may be difficult to cancel everything now, but because of what you are going through, it is still better to give up your relationship than go through marriage with all the doubts in your head. If there is still a chance left for you to postpone your wedding, do so and seek counsel. You may really need time to adjust to each other and get to know each other better.

When is the right time for guys to court and for girls to accept suitors?

"I am 13 years old and my suitor is 14. I feel so much flattered and I think I am falling in love. Many people say I am too young, but I think I am old enough to fall in love. Why can't I accept my suitor?"

Anyone who is ready to say "I love you" should also be ready to say "I am willing to marry you".

The Bible says, there is always a time for everything under the sun. Readiness is a factor of time. A person who is responsible enough to take care of her own personal needs physically, financially, emotionally and spiritually is most likely ready to enter a relationship. But if both of you still depend upon your parents for all these, we suggest that you wait and pray about it earnestly until the right time comes.

Consider also your priorities in life. Do you think that having a boyfriend or girlfriend at your age will not interfere with your studies or your spiritual growth? Entering a relationship should eventually and soon lead to settling down in marriage. Anyone who is ready to say "I love you" should also be ready to say "I am willing to marry you".

You are still both young. You have a lot of time to enjoy many things as a single. You can enjoy the pure fellowship and friendship of other young people like yourselves without any string attached. You have plenty of time to improve on yourself and be ready when the right time and person comes along. Be guided by God's Word. Do not let emotions overpower your sensible decision. Try to observe young married couples and compare yourself with them to find out if you are mature enough to handle relationships and eventually family life. Ask your parents' opinion, too. You are still under their covering anyway. And obey whatever they will tell you.

Courtship means responsibilities. One does not court just because it is fun, nor to prove that he is not a sissy, nor to satisfy the cravings of the flesh and the heart. When a guy begins to court, it means he is serious, mature and ready to settle down. Courtship is a step towards marriage. On the girl's part, it also means that anytime, she is ready to give up her single status to prepare herself to become a wife and eventually a mother.

Dear teen reader, allow us to ask you the following questions to find out if you or your sweetheart-to-be is ready. If you can answer the following questions with a resounding 'YES', then you are most probably ready to court and she, ready to accept suitors.

For Boys:

1) Are you disciplined and responsible enough to fix your bed every morning and help do household chores without being told? (Simple but true, right?)

2) Can you already wash and iron your own clothes?

3) When you say, "I love you" to the girl, are you ready to say, "Will you marry me?"

4) Are you ready to spend for gifts for the girl you are going to court out of your own pocket?

5) Are you independent enough so as not to ask from your parents money to date your girl?

6) Are you ready to give up your singlehood and your time with friends and your family?

7) Can you face the girl's parents and say that you have a stable job to support your girl when you get married?

8) Are you prepared for the responsibilities of married life such as shouldering the expenses for your wedding? And when you get married and have children, would you be able to buy your child milk, at least rent a house, feed your wife, pay for electrical and water bills?

9) Will you be ready to give up your studies and ambitions in order to find a job to support your family?

10) Will you be ready to do hard labor because if you have not finished your studies, that maybe the only job where you will qualify?

11) Are you willing to face future problems and intend to stick it out with your woman through hard times such as sicknesses, quarrels, disagreements, and other marital rows?

For Girls:
1) Are you responsible enough to do household chores such as cleaning the house, cooking, washing and ironing clothes, fixing your own bed, marketing and other chores?
2) When a guy says, "I love you", are you ready and willing to say, "I am willing to marry you"?
3) Are you willing to give up your privilege of not asking anything from your parents and not be under their responsibility as far as material needs are concerned?
4) Are you ready to give up your singlehood and your time with friends and your family?
5) Can you assure the guy's parents that you are able to care for all the needs of their son as much as they are able to do?
6) Are you ready to face the responsibilities of married life such as having children, taking care of the baby, waking up in the middle of the night to feed him, helping your husband earn money to buy your child milk and yourself food, at least rent a house, pay for electrical and water bills?
7) Will you be ready to give up your studies and ambitions in order to find a job to help support your family?
8) Are you willing to take on a job such as in factories, or as a househelper because those may be the only jobs undergraduates are qualified in?
9) Are you willing to stick it out with your man through hard times such as in sicknesses, quarrels, disagreements, and other marital rows?

You may not realize it, but your teen years is the time for preparation for a lifetime ahead of you. Do not be in such a hurry. Life has a lot to offer in every stage, especially if you belong to God.

3 How can I overcome fear in courtship?

> *"I want to court this girl of my fancy but I am so embarrassed, I do not know what to do or how to start. Sometimes I feel stupid. I also have this fear of rejection that if she would not accept, I would totally be at a loss. What should I do?"*

You need not be intimidated because courting can be an enjoyable experience. Relax. Courtship can be very fulfilling and rewarding. It is like saying to the girl 'I am offering myself to you, for you to know me better, with my strengths and imperfections. Likewise I want to know you.' This selfless act of reaching out is the essence of courtship. You are not on the receiving side, but more on the giving side. You give the person your attention, care, time, talents, individuality.[2] This is an opportune time to develop friendship.

The reason why some men are sometimes afraid to court is because they are not sure about the girl and about themselves as well. Readiness is very important. Therefore, before you make any move, you should really be doubly sure that the girl you will court is God's best and will for you. Once you are, then with God's help, it will not be as difficult as you imagine it.

Observe and look for opportunities when you can be together in group activities and where you can converse freely without being embarrassed. Talk about neutral things. Do not insist on your intentions at once. Make friends with her first.

Bro. Bong Baylon, former columnist of *Aglow* magazine gives us some practical tips:[3]

a) Avoid discussing serious matters at the beginning. Reserve "I love you's" for a more appropriate opportunity.

b) Practice a lot of humor in your conversations. This would put you both at ease.

c) Be sensitive to what is going on around you. Relate your stories to the most immediate experience common to you. Try revealing your values and thoughts concerning various subjects as you go along.

d) Be honest and sincere in your speech, and don't pretend to be somebody you are not. Encourage her also to be true to herself.

e) Take mental notes of the things she reveals about herself. Remember all these and when opportunities come to show some affection, like during her birthday, for instance, you would then be able to greet her effectively. If she just wants to be friends with you, respond properly as you meet her along that line.

Be patient. Pray to God for courage, wisdom and creativity. Remember to bring before Him every stage in your courtship and seek to honor Him. Allow Him to work freely in the girl's heart, better yet, allow God to court for you. With God on your side, who can be against you? Happy courting!

Is it proper for women to pursue men?

"I fell in love with this guy who treats me only as a friend. I know in my heart that I am going to marry him one day. My friends tell me we will look good together. Since I do not feel any encouragement from him, even though I feel he enjoys my company, my heart dictates that I write him a letter. My friends advised me that should he not respond, I will have to tell him straight to his face. Anyway, a lot of girls do this nowadays. Besides, I often see that on TV. I am just mounting some courage to do this and I feel a little guilty. But what if I lose him? Should I follow my heart's desire?"

The Bible says in Proverbs 18:22, "Blessed is the man who finds a wife." It is clear that the biblical standard for marriage is that it is the man who pursues the woman and not vice versa. Very often, men find women cheap and easy to get if they are the ones making themselves available. At times, men are turned off by the aggressiveness of some girls. A wrong move might prove detrimental to you. Why don't you just control your feelings and pray about it. If he is the one for you, the guy will surely find a way to win you; if not, God will give you the man He wills for you in due time if you are patient enough to wait.

5

What is wrong with matchmaking?

"I am 32 and still a bachelor. It is not that I am not interested in girls nor am I choosy with them. Rather, I have not found the right girl yet. My friends have been constantly teasing me, doing matchmaking with a lot of personable women. Because of embarrassment especially with the sister of my best friend, I was tempted to give in to his matchmaking schemes only because of pressure. My only problem is that I

do not feel she is the one for me. Please help me.”

Some Christians would call matchmaking as 'Charismatic witch-craft'. You do not have to give in to such pressure. You will only end up as the loser if you do not really love the girl and you do not feel she is God's will for you. Chances are you will not enjoy your marriage as compared to marrying God's best for you. Tell your friends to quit teasing you because it is not fair for you and the girl as well.

What is dating? Is it proper to date during courtship?

"I had a conservative upbringing. Because of pressure from my friends, I was forced to date a suitor and we went to a semi-lit restaurant by the bay. I got frustrated because towards the close of our date, he held my hand and tried to kiss me. I vehemently refused and I ran away from him. My friends laughed at me and mocked me when they learned about it. Now I have a new suitor who seems to behave properly. He is inviting me to attend a gospel concert. Is it a sin to date? Should I go out with him?"

Standing for what is right is never conservatism. You were right to refuse the guy in the first place. Do not succumb to peer pressure. Never mind if your friends dislike you for your values. Women like you ought not to entertain suitors who are overly aggressive, who cannot wait to date, hold your hands and kiss you. Stay away from those kinds. Keep yourself

Standing for what is right is never conservatism

pure. Pray that the guy you will marry will also maintain purity in his life and has the fear of God. Meanwhile, it is not really wrong to go out with your new suitor on a friendly date but be sure to have other people go with you. It would be much better if you refuse him so he will not misconstrue your action. Actually, dating is alright if it is done with the right person, at the right place and with the right attitude. Strictly speaking,

Pray that the guy you will marry will also maintain purity in his life...

this means that dating is activity for engaged couples and should be with the purpose of providing an opportunity for both parties to get to know each others likes, dislikes and interests.

Can the saying 'May the best man win' apply to me and my best friend?

> "My best friend and I have common interests in a lot of things, unfortunately even in the choice of a mate. I am planning to court this girl that I learned he also has interest in. Now we are keeping secrets from each other and somehow I feel a little distant to him. Shall I give way to him? How will I react towards him since we are not only friends, but are brothers in the Lord?"

It is not surprising that you share the same taste even with the woman you plan to court. It is therefore wise for you to really seek God first and find out if the girl is indeed God's will for you. If she is, you stand the chance of getting the woman you love because God will make a way for you to win her and then help your friend realize it. If not, then you will have to die to your flesh and quit. It is best to discuss the matter seriously with your friend and agree to pray about it together. Each of you should agree that this should not destroy your friendship.

How can you tell a flirt?

"I am very allergic to girls who are obviously attracting men's attention. But this girl I want to court appears to be hanging around with guys a lot. Although she flatters me at times, and seems to like me, I am not very sure about her. I am a one-woman-man and naturally, I want to be my girl's one and only. Is she only flirting with me? Do you think it is wise for me to court her?"

A flirt is one who plays at courtship. He or she only pretends and keeps the other party hanging. A flirt is either very selfish or insecure that is why he or she gets attention for himself or herself. This is also a sign of emotional immaturity and irresponsibility. In your case, she might only be leading you on and alluring you and yet may not have serious intentions. Try to investigate her background before making any major moves. If she is not the kind of girl who is serious with relationships, you might end up hurting yourself later. Check yourself as well. Are you just physically attracted to her or are you feeling something that will last in spite of…?

Here is what we suggest you do for the meantime. Be genuinely friendly with both girls and guys. Treat them as you would your sisters and brothers. Do not commit yourself to anyone as yet since you are still young. Wait and pray that God will lead you to the one who is best for you. Do not get involved with anyone if you do not have plans of pursuing marriage eventually. As for the girl, if you will have the chance to give her a brotherly advise, ask her to go to a Christian lady counselor who can help her.

❦ Chapter Six

ENGAGEMENT

ebster's dictionary defines engagement as "the act or state
of being engaged, pledged or committed to someone
in marriage".[1] The engagement period is an exciting
time as the couple officially announces to their loved ones and friends
and sometimes, even the general public that they are settling down
soon. Oftentimes, the guy gives his girl a ring (usually with one
stone thrust above the ring) to seal their engagement. The guy is
then referred to as the fiancé or beau. The girl is called fiancée. In
the Old Testament, engaged couples are called *betrothed* and are

considered married to one another.

When are couples considered as engaged?

"My boyfriend and I have been 'on' for 5 years and yet he never discussed about our marriage plans. I would always be the first one to bring it up and he would always reply to leave that to the future because he is busy with his business. Are we considered engaged?"

No, you are not considered engaged since you have not made any official or unofficial announcement that you are for each other. Being engaged means that you have or are planning to set up your wedding date. In your case, even at this point in time you are still uncertain whether he will marry you or not.

Five years is a bit too long to keep you hanging. We suggest that you talk to him seriously about his plans for your future. If his priority is his business, and would not discuss future plans with you, then you have the right to break off your commitment with him. It is abnormal for any relationship not to be heading towards engagement and eventually marriage. He has to agree on this or else you will have serious problems with him if this is not resolved first.

How long should an engagement be?

"Do you favor long engagement? We have been engaged for more than two years now and it seems that we are not yet prepared for marriage due to lack of finances and other considerations. We keep on dating but we are experiencing some serious sexual problems. I already committed to him even my body. My boyfriend is so aggressive and would get mad at me if I don't give in to his demands. What shall I do?"

No, we don't favor nor encourage long engagement. It would be ideal to be engaged between 6 months to 1 year. The purpose of entering into an engagement is to prepare for marriage. Long engagement poses danger due to over familiarity, too much closeness, and physical intimacy which goes beyond kissing, necking and petting. In many occasions, engaged couples lose control, and as in your case, commit fornication. These are sexual sins of immorality and fornication which God hates according to Galatians 5:19-21 and 1 Thessalonians 4:3-5.

We encourage you to maintain purity in your relationship. If you honor God, his favor will rest upon you, you will see His glory and people will be blessed by your relationship. You can still change and be restored at this stage if you are willing, by confessing and repenting of all lust and sexual sins. Then agree to refrain from any form of physical intimacy or sexual contact, like necking, petting or fornication until marriage. Set your own guidelines in dating and make sure you will respect and implement them.

3 What preparations are necessary during the engagement period?

"We heard you speak in a seminar. Can you please elaborate on the preparations you mentioned that we need to go through as a newly engaged couple?"

We encourage engaged couples to prepare themselves in all aspects of their lives: physically, materially, emotionally, socially and above all, spiritually.

Physically: Since married life is full of responsibilities, each of you has to make your body healthy especially in preparation for bearing children. Do regular exercises and work outs. Eat healthy foods and have a balance diet. Before we got married, I (Cynthia) was not used to eating vegetables and drinking milk, but I had to learn and force myself. I did not have any exercise regimen, so I took up basic swimming lessons, knowing that my husband-to-be loves to swim. It will be burdensome if one of the mates is sickly and is not able to cope with the strains of married life.

Prepare your body physically - your hair nicely kept, your nails always trimmed, your skin glowing in health and always try to smell fresh and clean. Be careful with your choice of clothes and perfume. This is not a time for the girl to wear revealing clothes. This is the time she should all the more be modest in her physical appearance.

Materially: You need money to sustain your family. So as a couple, you should really strive to use your resources wisely, save up and prepare for expenses for the wedding and thereafter. Try to live within your budget for the wedding preparations. The ceremony need not be elaborate and expensive. Simple rites will do, as long as you can afford it. Do not spend all your money for the wedding. Set aside some of it as your start up budget after the wedding.

Emotionally: Since engagement is an exciting period, you as a couple can get emotionally high, too. Because it is close to marriage, you feel and sense the closeness or belongingness and there is impending danger to become too intimate. It is during this time that couples often lose their balance and they fall into fornication. Guard your emotions. Remember that each of you doesn't yet have the right over each other's body. Keep away from places that are too romantic for comfort. Keep yourselves busy and always count the days so that you will be both willing to wait a little more.

Several couples I (Dante) ministered to and whose weddings I officiated really maintained purity in every stage of their relationship. Three of them experienced their first kiss only on their wedding day. The only form of intimacy they allowed during engagement was holding of hands. They preserved the culmination of their intimacy on their wedding night. They are living witnesses to the fact that it is possible to control their emotions and wait until it is time to fully express them. They can all testify that their wedding kiss and their first union were the sweetest things that happened to them. More experienced couples agree that this kind of relationship is bound to last till death.

Socially: Even as an engaged couple, you should not isolate your loved ones, friends and church brethren. Oftentimes, couples become exclusive to themselves that everything revolves around them and all others fade into the background. Remember that they care for you, too and are willing to help you when you need them. Develop relationships especially among would-be-in-laws. This will endear you more to them.

Spiritually: Engagement is the time to be more grateful to and dependent upon God and show that you love Him more than your partner. This is also a time for you as partners, to draw closer to God by praying together as often as possible. Bring to God all of your needs. Have Him bless every step of the preparation. Put Him at the center of your relationship. Being close to Him will also draw you away from temptations of immorality and sin. As you honor Him, you will find that blessings will overflow.

 ### What activities can couples engage in when they go on dates?

"I would like to have more meaningful dates with my girl. What should I do? Where should I take her?"

Here are some pointers:

a) Have definite plans where to go, what to discuss, what time to be back home. You should always bear in mind to glorify God even in your dating.

b) Go on group dates. It is safe to go in numbers so that temptations cannot set in. This goes true even for engaged couples. Being alone for long hours without interruptions can be dangerous and tempting.

c) Pray and ask people to cover you in prayer. Before you go on a date, pray that you both will seek to honor God in your dating.

d) Prepare physically. The man and the woman should present

themselves well. If you want to wear perfume, choose a mild one - not to attract or seduce but to show good grooming. Wear appropriate clothes that are not revealing to avoid seducing your fiancée. Remember, you are after true love and not lust.

e) Prepare financially, especially the guys. Make sure you have enough money for the date. Remember to live within your means.

f) Ask permission from parents or elders. Let them know where you are going and what time you will be home. If you are the guy and you do this to the parents of the girl, for sure they will appreciate you and will respect you more.

g) Avoid going into dark places, like cinemas, darkly lit parks and the like. Never stay too long inside your car doing nothing. These places offer too much temptations for lust, immorality and fornication to breed.

h) Try your best not to spend too long hours alone especially in places where there will be no interruptions. Guys should never sleep over the house of their girlfriends and vice-versa.

i) Control yourself by avoiding physical contact, except for gentle-manly gestures and conformity to etiquette.

j) Set and agree on some guidelines; like activities to do together, topics to discuss such as future plans, likes and dislikes, when to go on date and how often and other concerns in your relationship.

k) Be creative in your dating. You can go to concerts, or watch games together, pray or study God's word together, or even attend church activities together.

l) Communicate openly. Develop transparent verbal expressions of emotions, ideas and concerns making sure that godly values are adhered to.

 What are some of the things engaged couples need to talk and discuss about before marriage?

> *"My fiancée is coming back from abroad after two years and we are planning to get married in one month's time. We have been away from each other and I know we have a lot of catching up to do. Could you remind me of the important things that I need to know about and discuss with her?"*

We always encourage our counselees to open up and be transparent to their partners. We advise them to confess every unfaithfulness and settle each one of them before they get married. We tell them to be open to forgive no matter what happened in the past so that they can have a clean slate and a fresh start. Here are some more suggestions on things for discussions:

a) Your present and future plans individually and as a couple

b) Your likes and dislikes or preferences in food, manner of dressing, use of time, entertainment, investments, etc.

c) Common interests in business, sports, etc.

d) Health conditions (tell the truth if you will not be able to bear a child, or if there is any artificial part or abnormality in your body)

e) Your family background, good or bad

f) Your profession or church ministry involvement – as to whether you can pursue them or not after marriage

g) Advancement in career or further studies

h) Detailed wedding plans and preparations

i) Place of abode after the wedding

j) Jobs or livelihood projects or business to venture into

k) Number of children desired and whether or not to have babies immediately or use of birth control

l) Views on sex and its fulfillment and practice

m) Relationship and dealing with in-laws and friends, especially in the area of extending material help

n) Treatment of each other or behavior in public or in a social gatherings

o) Establishing priorities for the family or household affairs

p) Church to attend if each comes from a different one and where to give their tithes

q) Budget for the wedding and after

r) Sharing of household chores

We discussed some of these ourselves before we got married. For instance we agreed that when we have disagreements we will not involve or run to our in-laws or relatives for problems. We would settle our problems ourselves with the help of God. We knew of an elderly couple who told us that on their wedding night they drew lots as to who will put on the mosquito net before they go to sleep and who will wash the dishes. The one who drew the lot will do it until death. The husband passed away after they were married for 55 years, but until that day he was the one who put on the mosquito net.

We hope these will help eliminate little misunderstandings and make your adjustment period easier and much more bearable. Happy wedding!

Are those into mutual understanding (MU) also considered engaged?

> *"My best friend and I hit it off together. Many people say that we are like two peas in a pod. When he has a family gathering, he would always invite me. I also introduce him to my folks as my best friend. He also takes me along during their office outing and gatherings. Many times when he wants to go to the mall, he would*

> *ask me to accompany him. A lot of people read something deeper in our relationship but we never talk about our feelings towards each other. Some of my friends tell me that there are at least two guys who are interested to court me but could not make the first move because of my best friend. I am afraid to ask because it might destroy our friendship. Is our relationship what other people say "mutual understanding"?*

Mutual understanding is described as a mutual admiration or attraction felt by a person toward another and is reciprocated by the other. This relationship does not involve courtship and has no permanent commitment. Your case fits into this category. You cannot bank on this relationship because of lack of genuine commitment; you only have false hopes. This is dangerous especially if you become deeply attracted in the flesh. It is not fair for both of you because there is no plan of marriage involved. When the relationship turns sour the bond breaks apart. You will be on the losing end.

It is therefore wise that you open up to him and define your relationship. In this way, any soul ties with him will be severed and then you will be free to know God's will for yourself. You may start by asking him, "If you were in my place, how would you answer our friends asking about the two of us?" The answer will clearly define your relationship.

Is counseling a must for engaged couples before the wedding?

> *"My parents are born again Christians. My fiancée and I sometimes get invited to their church and they highly recommend us to go through counseling with their pastor. If we are amenable, the pastor is also willing to officiate our wedding. What can we expect from this?"*

The marriage counselor, whether a pastor or not, is an experienced person who has, by the grace of God, gained expertise in counseling couples to help them establish a successful marriage. Taking time to consult him now would minimize future problems. We encourage you to go through this process. You will surely not regret it.

Here is one advantage. At one time, we were counseling a couple before their marriage and during the third session together, we asked that we counsel in the presence of their parents. We discussed about transparency in all things including money matters, that each should know how much they are earning. The engaged couple were nudging each other and we were glad it was truly witnessing in their spirits. Later they told us, it was a *rhema* word not only for them but their parents as well. The guy's father who has been married to his wife for 30 years still kept his salary secret.

At another time we were counseling a couple about being transparent, we asked if there is anything that each of them would like each other to improve and deal with. The guy said, "I am pissed off whenever her shopping takes too long." The girl said, "I do not like the way he handles his money and we need to discuss about helping his relatives." That day, they learned things they needed to improve on. They have been married for three years now, and by God's grace they have not experienced any major problem in their relationship.

Some of the things that we ourselves discuss during marriage counseling are establishing proper guidelines such as discussed in the preceding question, which includes how to resolve future conflicts in their relationship, proper sex practice, birth control and other problems that they might be currently undergoing.

From our experience in counseling we have observed that those who have undergone marriage counseling are the ones whose marriages are more stable. And those who have not, usually suffer much in marriage and worse, some end up in broken relationships.

What is an engagement vow?

> *"When my wife and I first came to you for counseling, you made us realize the importance of an engagement vow. My father is also a pastor, can I recommend to him to do the same to those he will counsel for marriage?"*

Surely you can. There is no copyright to this because it came from the Holy Spirit. I remember the first time I asked my counselees to recite the engagement vow, they were both crying because prior to that the Lord revealed to me that they have been committing fornication. They confessed their sins and were willing to change after that. Indeed, they remained true to this vow and they respected each other's body and walked in holiness. During their wedding day, the presence of the Lord was so strong and the couple were exuberant.

This engagement vow came about when the Lord gave me the insight that if couples recite their wedding vows before God and other witnesses, then it is also proper for them to make a vow not to touch each other till wedding night. They will not engage in kissing, necking, petting, or sexual union before marriage. They will vow to love, respect and honor each other and vow not to sin against God. I have found this very effective among the couples who have in the recent years asked me to officiate their wedding.

Should difference in religion stand in the way of my engagement?

> *"I was the one you ministered to in Bahrain. If you remember I shared with you that I got born again only 2 years ago while I was in Qatar. I wrote to propose marriage to my girlfriend and she accepted, so we got engaged. After that I got convicted by the Holy Spirit to share Jesus to her. I was so surprised and sorry about her response.*

> *She said she will only marry me if I give up my religion and that she will never be born again. What should I do?"*

Religion is a major factor to consider in marriage, although being born again is not a religion but a relationship with Jesus. We know of several broken relationships that resulted from these differences. The Bible says in Amos 3:3, "How can the two walk together unless they agree?" It is a matter of your choice now. The ball is in your hands. If your faith and love for God weighs more to you than her, then it will be easy for you to decide.

You are struggling because you are contemplating on two choices. We suggest that you lay this problem aside first and deepen your relationship with God. Get to know Him more and He will be the one to direct you. If your girlfriend breaks your engagement, then you are off the responsibility. Meanwhile, pray for her that she may be enlightened.

What medical tests should engaged couples undergo before marriage?

> " *My wedding date is two months from now. I read from an American wedding magazine that it is a common practice for engaged couples to undergo medical examination and treatment. Please confirm this for us."*

It is always wise to have a medical check-up before getting married. Doctors can advise how you can be both physically fit because getting married is such a big responsibility. There should be no surprises. Each partner has the right to know the physical condition or illnesses that his/her partner suffer from. You should also be tested for fertility and *rh* blood factor compatibility. If your blood is not *rh* compatible, then the doctor can advise you what to expect or do. If one partner has inability to bear children, it is fair for the other to be prepared for it.

11

What is wrong with live-in arrangements?

"We are a couple living together without going through the ceremony. We are so in love and believe that ours is as good as any married couple's because we are committed to each other. Why do some people scorn at us?"

A live-in arrangement is like a trial marriage. It doesn't stand on solid ground because there is no commitment, no obligation required, no legal foundation and most of all, no blessing from above. Once the live-in couple realize that they are not suited for each other, or if they fall out of love for each other and find someone else, they simply call it quits. There is no stability in this arrangement.

There are many other negative sides to a live–in partnership. Spiritually speaking, such a relationship brings curse because it is a sin. This will bring much strife in the family because of the lack of permanency in the structure of the family. Legally, children born out of this relation has no legal name of their own and therefore have no legal benefits.

Author Evelyn Feliciano, writes, "there is no fairness or equality in live-in. The girl usually comes out the loser. She has allowed herself to be sexually used and perhaps abused. Besides, when the love affair falls apart and it begets children, they are left to the mother. I know some single mothers struggling to raise their fatherless children while keeping a steady job. The tremendous emotional strain and social stigma sap the strength and courage and dignity of the one-parent family. It may be fashionable these days but it is not worth emulating."[2]

For God, marriage is a sacred and holy thing. He doesn't want the marriage bed defiled and He judges those who are immoral. Hebrews 13:4.

Facing Reality...

12

How does one cope if his/her partner breaks the engagement off?

"My partner and I were preparing for our wedding. We were already working on our house and its furnishings. We have opened our joint bank account and have set the date, the wedding outfit, the invitation, the venue of the rites and the reception and honeymoon. All of a sudden my fiancé halted all preparations and asked for a cool off period saying that he needed more time to think about his decision to marry me, hoping that I wouldn't mind. Weeks and months went by without any word from him while I cried my heart out. Then he called to say, we were not meant for each other. A few months later, he married another woman. How can anyone possibly cope with this kind of situation, especially if you love your mate so much?"

There is no one who can comfort you more than God Himself. Go ahead and cry to God and tell Him how it hurts. Spend a lot of time with Him because more than anyone else, He alone can understand and heal your wounds. Remember that all things work together for the good of them that love God and who are called according to His purpose (Romans 8:28). The sun will rise again. A new dawn will break forth. It may not be easy at first but you will survive. Tell yourself that there is no use in reliving the past. Look to the future. Start afresh. Fellowship with your family and friends more. Give yourself to love other people. Get busy with the work God has entrusted to you but do not close your heart to anyone who would want to consider you as his partner. God has someone better. You can be happy as you serve Him alone.

13

How should you handle the engagement if you find someone else?

"I am engaged to be married in a matter of months. We have had this relationship for the last four years before we decided to get married. I am now having second thoughts about it because I do not feel I love my fiancé that much to spend the rest of my life with him. I fear, however, that it will be a big issue among our families and friends. But you see, I met this man who told me that he believes God has something for both of us. I think I am falling for him each day. I sought the Lord about it because I do not want to hurt my boyfriend. I am getting signs that I should not go ahead with the marriage plans. Am I going to sin if I break off or should I just go ahead as planned? Please help me."

The first thing to do is to make sure that it is not infatuation that you feel for this second man. You really have to confirm from God who between the two is His will for you. We suggest that you fast and pray and spend time away from both your fiancé and the new guy. Seek counsel. Although it will cause some trouble to cancel everything, it is wiser to break off your engagement than to spend the rest of your life being unhappy with the wrong guy. The break-up may cause many hurts but your wrong decision may be even worse.

"*Love*
is an ocean
of emotions
entirely surrounded
by expenses."

- Lord Dewar

🌷Chapter Seven

WEDDING PREPARATIONS

By Nel Ferido - De Guzman

G od is absolutely fond of preparations! He must have enjoyed preparing the grand master plan of His precious and marvelous project down to its making - hailed as "The Creation". Looking closely at His work, one is caught in deep awe and amazement that not one part is lacking or misplaced. Not one detail is in disarray. The very keen-eyed Creator made and positioned every part, even the very minute details, in beautiful and perfect order.

Note: Sis. Nel, our guest writer is an Event & Wedding Planner/Coordinator. She used to hold her own office, Times and Seasons Event Planner, in Tandang Sora, Quezon City, Philippines until she got married in April, 2001. She has coordinated weddings for foreigners, socialites, churchmates, close friends and relatives—with budgets ranging from few thousand pesos to hundreds of thousands. She has also coordinated debut parties and corporate events (product launching). She now does consultations on event planning and can be reached through JHMT at (632) 438-1819 to 21 (e-mail: tong_nel@yahoo.com).

Nel is very much enthusiastic and loves her new role in life—that is being a wife to Ernie. They are now concentrating on a new business in website development.

God is absolutely fond of weddings, too! In fact, this was His idea. In Genesis 2:18, He already knew of Adam's need of a woman before the first man could ever thought of needing one...and God was all prepared for it.

He placed within Adam a mysterious longing, something which the first man could not quite understand. Even after naming all the living creatures, a task that God directed him to do, the longing was still there. Adam could not explain what it was and why it won't disappear. One day, God perceived that Adam was ready. At the perfect moment, at the right place and at the right time God brought before his very eyes the answer·he has been searching for and which not one of the other creations could supply. Adam realized "this one" is different from the rest. This one matches him! Adam saw Eve and exclaimed in utter amazement, "*This is now bone of my bones, and flesh of my flesh...(Genesis 2:23)*". "*Alas, this one now corresponds me!*" What a wonderful moment for Adam! He was feeling ecstatic! He was humbled and thankful to God who provided for his need. The very first garden wedding took place in the Garden of Eden with God as the principal witness.

God topbilled Genesis with the unique and beautiful love story of Adam and Eve and closes in the book of Revelations with another marriage celebration—the grand marriage supper of the Lamb with the saints in joy and triumph!

Weddings touch the very heart of the Father and what a way =to emphasize this truth when we read in the Gospel how He permitted the first miracle of Jesus to take place in a wedding. Such are not coincidence! God truly loves weddings and He wills every marriage to last.

It is said that the wedding day is the happiest occasion in a man and woman's life. To assist the bride and groom take pleasure in preparing for this much-awaited event in their lives, the following frequently asked questions (FAQ's) will lend them a helping hand in making their wedding a day to cherish and remember. It is our hope that this will help you plan and prepare down to the particulars. May you gain the confidence to be the wedding planner/coordinator of your very own wedding. Enjoy and have fun!

What are the "first things first" in wedding preparations?

> *"My fiancé and I have plans of getting married next year. We would like to start off the preparations a year ahead. What are the things we need to accomplish first?"*

First and foremost, before commencing with the preparations, be sure that you are both committed to live for each other the rest of your lives. Ask yourself, *"Will you be willing to spend the remainder of your years with your fiancé discounting his/her unpredictable mood swings and weaknesses?"* If your answer is a solid *"Yes*, I can live with him/her through thick and thin (*'kaya ko siyang pakisamahan'*)" and still love him/her despite all these flaws, then you are ready to get married!

The second most important thing to do is to PRAY together. Ask the Holy Spirit for guidance and wisdom in every step of the wedding preparations.

The Price of Wedding

Thirdly, it is imperative that you immediately set the date and time of your wedding. Setting it early will give you a better chance of getting your dream ceremony and reception sites. Because the more famous churches and reception venues are usually booked a year before, it is best that you finalize the day of the wedding as early as you can. But have two or three alternative dates in case the day you have in mind is already booked.

When selecting the date, you can be guided by family affairs (birthdays, anniversaries), holidays (Christmas day, New Year's day, etc.), special events (Mother's Day, Father's Day, Valentine's Day, etc.) and tourist activities (Asian Games, Olympics, etc.) that will take place. Bear in mind that in some of these special days, prices of commodities like flowers, even hotel accommodations, etc. may increase. Consider also that traffic condition is worst during the Christmas shopping season or Valentine's Day. In our country, the weather condition from June till December is very unpredictable. The time of your wedding will determine how formal it will be. The rule of the thumb is the later in the day the wedding is, the more formal it is likely to be.

This early, you may want to discuss with your fiancé the possibility of hiring a wedding planner/coordinator to handle the preparations. The coordinator can do everything for you ("worry-free" type of wedding) or he could help you out on some of the preparations or just be there on the day itself. At least at the outset, you will know the extent of the actual planning and actual work you will expend for your big day. Whether you will be the one to accomplish everything with the help of your close friends and relatives or you will let the coordinator do everything for you.

What is *pamanhikan* or *pedida de mano*?

"I already informed my parents of our plan to settle down. Now, I want to formally ask my girlfriend's hand from my future in-laws. How should I go about it?"

For the Filipinos, formally asking for the hand of the bride in marriage is called *pamanhikan*. In Spanish it is called *pedida de mano*. *Pamanhikan* which literally means "climbing the stairs" or figuratively, "visiting the betrothed" is customarily done when the groom's family calls upon the family of the bride to request for her hand in marriage.

Traditionally, on the day of the *pamanhikan*, the bride's family prepares food for the occasion while the groom's family brings its share of food to the bride's home. A *padrino* (or "advocate"), if ever there's one, also joins this very important dinner conversation. Details about the marriage plans are discussed like the date, number of guests and principal sponsors. The decision on who will shoulder the wedding expenses as well as the place for newlyweds to start their home, are also agreed upon. This is also the most opportune time when both families, especially the future in-laws, get to know each other. It is part of the tradition for the groom to send fresh flowers to his future bride and future mother-in-law in the morning of the day of the *pamanhikan*; towards the end of the *pamanhikan*, the future mother-in-law presents the bride with the engagement ring or privately the groom surprises his future bride with it. [1]

Nowadays, when time is gold and the couple would want to get rid of the hassles of the preparation, an alternative is to have the *pamanhikan* in a cozy restaurant where sumptuous food is readily available or to get a reputable caterer to prepare the sit down dinner. In the western culture, *pamanhikan* is equivalent to Parent's Dinner.

3 What is the *despedida de soltera*?

> "We just had the 'pamanhikan', and my family is insisting to host an occasion where my fiancé will be formally welcomed to our family. When do we do this?"

The *despedida de soltera* (DDS) which means "farewell to maidenhood", "is a symbolic gesture of consent by the bride's family to her future husband". [2] It is the occasion when the bride's family host a luncheon or dinner to formally welcome their future son-in-law to their family. It is scheduled a week or two before the wedding day. Aside from the immediate family members, the presence of the wedding sponsors and close friends will make this event special. A short program may also be prepared the highlight of which is when the father of the bride offers a toast and offers his good wishes to his future son-in-law; the groom immediately returning the favor also offers a toast to his bride.

The equivalent of this occasion in the western culture is the rehearsal dinner.[3]

What is the bridal shower and the stag party?

"My boyfriend and I are both Bible-believers and will be getting married next month. However, our officemates who are mostly unbelievers told us that they will give us a stag party and a bridal shower respectively. Knowing their lifestyles and way of thinking, should we say 'yes' to them? I'm afraid for myself and my fiancé to go because I have heard lots of mischievous things taking place at this kind of party (like hiring of

The Stag Party

female and male entertainers). Since declining is not a polite thing to do, how should we make it clear to them that we only go for 'wholesome' bridal shower and stag party?"

"The idea of a bridal shower goes back many centuries to the Netherlands when a poor Dutch miller fell in love with a rich maid. The maid's father disapproved of the marriage and refused to provide a dowry. The miller's friends got together and 'showered' the couple with items that would help them establish a household. Thus, the bridal shower was born."[4]

A bridal or wedding shower is usually a party given to the bride by her female family members and close friends including staff or other colleagues. As a rule, the bride gives the hostess the guests list including their addresses and contact numbers. If there is more than one shower, the bride should divide and group the guests among the parties. It will be too expensive for the guests to bring presents to every of the bride's shower. Normally, those invited at the shower party are invited to the wedding. But there would be occasions when a shower party is given to the bride but not all attendees are invited to the wedding, e.g. a shower party thrown by officemates.[5] Showers can have themes (e.g. kitchen gadgets for a kitchen theme, lingerie for a honeymoon theme, miscellaneous showers for anything) so gifts "showered" to the bride are expected to relate to the theme. The highlight of the shower is the opening of gifts. Games are incorporated in the party and refreshments are served after the opening of gifts. Nowadays, it is common to have couple's shower hosted for the bride and the groom.

The groom's best man and male friends usually give the stag party or what is commonly known as the bachelor's party. Recommended wholesome activities for the stag party may vary from involving in a common hobby or sports like fishing, swimming or just gathering together for a sumptuous meal.

The bridal shower and stag party take place a few days before the wedding day primarily to celebrate the upcoming marriage. This is also the time when friends would like to enjoy the company of the bride and groom in the last few days of their singlehood. At the party, the married friends can give advises on the "how to's" of married life.

In your case, be frank and firm on your stand and convictions. If you haven't shared to them the Gospel, do so. Tell your officemates that you will only take part in wholesome activities and you will not engage in malicious games of any kind. A small party gathering in a nearby restaurant will be ok and fine for both of you to attend. In this way, you will be able to spend time with them and appreciate the preparations they did. Also, this arrangement will keep both of you safe and guarded from any surprises and untoward happenings that you may regret later.

5 What is a dowry?

"My parents are old-fashioned and still adhere to the custom of asking for a dowry during the 'pamanhikan'. How can I tell them without hurting their feelings that there will be no dowry, but instead my fiancé will be the one to shoulder most of the wedding expenses?"

Our ancestors practiced asking for a dowry (in the form of a piece of land, gold, money, or anything of high-value) from the man who wants to marry their daughter. Though asking for a dowry is no longer a common practice, its influence is evident in our culture and tradition since the groom usually takes care of the total wedding expenses.

In a very polite and respectful manner, explain to your parents that your fiancé's act of of shouldering most of the wedding expenses is actually the equivalent of dowry in modern times. Explain, too, that he is also sincere in his intentions and very responsible to take this major step.

In our country nowadays, the wedding cost is shared by the couple. There would be instances, however, when parents gift the couple with cash money that will help in their wedding expenses.

6 What are the ways to have a practical wedding?

"We do not want an elaborate wedding ceremony because we want to be practical. Besides, we really do not have that much budget. What could be our other alternatives?"

I know for a fact that in every woman's heart, there is a picture of a dream wedding. And this dream wedding can come true without hurting the pocket.

There are myriad ways on how to cut down on your wedding expenses. Cutting down on food cost which has an average 60% share on the total wedding costs will certainly keep your expenses to a minimum. Keeping down the food cost will mean keeping the guest list small. You can set up your wedding at home where only your immediate and close family members are the invited guests. You can also have both the ceremony and reception setup in your church (if space would allow it). For a garden wedding, you can rent a smaller venue which can hold the ceremony and reception combined. The rent will be comparatively lower than well-known and upscale venues. A civil wedding is certainly not out of the options. After all, what really matters is that you wed the man of your dreams (be sure he is the one God has prepared for you), and surely God will bless the day you have been dreaming of.

7 Do you have a checklist for wedding planning?

"Because of our budget constraints, we can't afford to hire a wedding planner and would like to do the preparations ourselves. How should we go about this? Is there a checklist you can give us as a guide?"

Use the checklist in preparing for your wedding:

TO DO's	IDEAL TIME LINE
Select the date	6 mo. - 1 yr. before
- Have 2-3 alternative dates as options (in case site, officiant in mind is already booked)	
- Consider weather condition when selecting the date (in tropical countries marrying during summer time or rainy season?, in the West - is it winter, spring, summer or fall wedding?)	
Talk about your budget	6 mo. - 1 yr. before
- Number of guests	
- Set priorities (will spend more for photos and videos than food?)	
- Are you going to hire a wedding coordinator?	
Schedule *pamanhikan*	6 mo. - 1 yr. before
Buy a comprehensive wedding organizer	6 mo. - 1 yr. before
Publish the engagement / wedding announcement in the local newspaper or post the announcement online	2 mo. - 1 yr. before
Reserve ceremony and reception sites	6 mo. - 1 yr. before
- Decide on the kind of wedding (garden wedding, church wedding, beach wedding, etc.)	

TO DO's	IDEAL TIME LINE

- When choosing the sites, consider where the bulk of the guests will be coming from, also the place/hotel where you will be changing
- Do they have provision for a generator in case of brownout?

Scout for a caterer   6 mo.- 1 yr. before
- Get quotation from at least 3 suppliers so you can compare prices
- Take a look at the pictures of their past functions so you'll have an idea on their kind of preparations
- Decide: is it buffet or sit-down?
- Schedule food tasting

Draw up guest list   6 mo. before
- Select the principal sponsors
- Select the attendants / members of the rest of the entourage
- Name the remaining guests in your list (relatives, friends, officemates, churchmates, former schoolmates, etc.)

Choose and book your officiating minister   6 mo. before
- Discuss the contents of the wedding program or readings for the ceremony
- Consult him if you have plans to have your own vows

TO DO's	IDEAL TIME LINE
Print the invitation	6 mo. before

- Check samples of reputable printers to pick up ideas
- Think of the wordings
- Carefully proofread (especially the spelling of the names of the bridal entourage
- Select color of ink, type and thickness of paper, font type, style, printing process
- Prepare direction cards/map of the ceremony and reception sites , indicate major transportation services available en route to the ceremony and reception site (for those commuting)
- You may want to have the wedding program and thank-you cards printed

Contact a calligrapher	4 - 6 mo. before

- In case you want a professional to do the addressing of the invitations (but can do w/o a calligrapher)

Order bridal gown including accessories (headdress, veil, gloves, arrhae, shoes, garter, money bag, etc.) and dress of entourage	6 mo. before

- Choose the color motif
- Buy bridal magazines to help you in conceptualizing the design
- Window-shop at showrooms of reputable couturiers, bridal salon and stores to gather ideas

TO DO's	IDEAL TIME LINE

- Attend bridal shows (normally conducted for free)

Purchase groom's attire   6 mo. before

Schedule for the engagement   6 mo. before
seminar/ counseling seminar
with the officiating minister

Choose photographer   6 mo. before
- Look at sample works
- Study the package
- Submit a shotlist (you think is impt.) you want to add to the regular list
- Candid or posed shots?
- Schedule for the wedding portrait
- Choose between sepia, black-and-white or color photography
- Who will own the negatives?
- Discuss costings for recopy

Book videographer   6 mo. before
- Review past works
- Study the package
- Give the pictures to be included in the video

Name your florist   6 mo. before
- Discuss flower arrangements and kind of flowers to be used
- Give swatch of color motif to serve as guide for the selection of flowers

TO DO's	IDEAL TIME LINE
Choose your sound system supplier	6 mo. before
Book musicians	6 mo. before
- Choose musical selections you want to play during the ceremony (prelude, processional, interlude, recessional) and reception	
Book band for the reception	6 mo. before
- Choose songs you want played	
Find a hair and make-up artist you're comfortable with	2 - 6 mo. before
- Schedule for a trial make-up	
- Have pictures taken after the trial so you'll see how you look with this kind of hair and make-up style	
Finalize "honeymoon" plans	1 - 6 mo. before
- Is honeymoon destination local or abroad?	
- Confer with travel agent	
- Prepare for requirements for honeymoon abroad (passport, visa, medical exam, inoculation and other paper requirements)	
- Buy honeymoon outfit, etc.	
Apply for a marriage license	3 mo. before
- Prepare the requirements (see item no. 10)	

TO DO's	IDEAL TIME LINE
Rent bridal car or horse-drawn carriage or whatever kind of vehicle the bride will use	3 mo. before
Distribute the invitation	2 mo. before
Order your wedding cake	2 mo. before
- Choose design and type of cake (fondant, buttercake, etc.) in accordance with color motif and theme of the wedding	
Order the wedding bands	2 mo. before
- Think of the inscription	
- Have it engraved	
Enlist in a bridal registry	2 mo. before
Buy gifts for parents, principal sponsors, entourage, officiating minister and **give-aways/wedding favors** for the guests	1 mo. before
Order other stuff needed:	1 mo. before
- Stockings & other special lingerie gown requires	
- Wedding Bible	
- Unity candle	
- Guest book	
- Signature frame/message cards	
- Decorated basket to hold the give-aways	
- Decorated clip board to hold the marriage contract	
- Plum or special sign pen (optional)	

- Specialized wine glass (optional)
- Specialized cake cutter & knife (optional)
- Materials for recessional (nuptial bubbles, snowflakes, poppers, confetti, etc.)
- Rent or borrow mannequin

Break-in wedding shoes	1 mo. before
Visit your dermatologist and dentist	1 mo. before
Check-up with the doctor	1 mo. before
Have final dress fitting - Distribute the dresses	2 weeks before
Book room where you will change	2 weeks before
Attend *despedida de soltera*, **bridal shower/stag party**	2 weeks before
Attend the wedding rehearsal - Confirm attendance - Prepare food and drinks for the rehearsal	1-2 weeks before
Ask someone to do telephone brigade for those who did not respond (R.S.V.P.)	1-2 weeks before
Arrange transportation and accommodation for out-of-town guests	1-2 weeks before
Finalize reception programme	

TO DO's	IDEAL TIME LINE

- Assign an emcee
- Finalize sequence of the programme — 1-2 weeks before

Hire traffic officer, if necessary — 1-2 weeks before

Brief the wedding party and other people concerned of their responsibilities — 1 week before
- Maid of Honor and Best Man during the ceremony
- Best Man to offer the tributary toast during the reception
- Who will distribute the wedding program, Bible, ring, etc.
- Who will hand out the corsage and boutonnieres
- Who will announce the "order of photographs"
- Who will distribute souvenirs (guests and sponsors)
- Guest book attendant
- In-charge of the signature frame
- Who will submit the marriage contract
- Who will bring the gifts at home
- Who will be the transportation coordinator (security and parking)

Notify caterer of final headcount — 1 week before
- Prepare place cards and table numbers

Finalize floor plan and seat arrangement — 1 week before

TO DO's	IDEAL TIME LINE
Write personal vows and memorize	1 week before
Choose wedding-day jewelries	1 week before
Ask somebody to remind the suppliers (make-up artist, sound system, musician, caterer, transpo, etc.) of the date and time of their appointment	3 days before
Remind participants of ceremony of their roles (lector, readers, offerors)	3 days before
Confirm travel arrangements	
- Pack for honeymoon	3 days before
- Prepare what to bring for honeymoon abroad (passport/visa, photo ID, adapter for small appliances, health and credit cards, check book, first-aid kit, essential toiletries	

Note : Please refer to Lovelife Vol. 2 for more details about honeymoon

Have a relaxing facial and body massage, pedicure and manicure	1-2 days before
Delegate check-up of venue of ceremony and reception	on or before the day itself
- Check arrangements and decoration	

- Test sound system and
  sequence of musical selections

Eat a good breakfast, RELAX and ENJOY THIS DAY!

After the reception, be sure to do the ff:
- Double-check if all the pages of the marriage
  contract are completely signed. Remind the assigned
  person to submit the marriage contract within the
  required fifteen-day period
- Pay the balance (if any) to the supplier concerned
- Give the "tip"
- Pack the left-over food (if this was agreed upon with the
  caterer)
- Gather all the wedding paraphernalia (guest book,
  message cards, signature frame, etc.)
- Transport gifts to home
- Return all borrowed and rented materials

What should be the sequence of activities for the wedding ceremony and reception?

"I'm writing down the sequence of my wedding cereemony and the program for my reception. Can you please give me a sample from which I could base my outline?"

I advise you to consult first your officiating minister for the outline of your wedding ceremony. He might have his own style of officiating the rites. If there is none, you can use the sample sequence of the wedding ceremony below. If you plan to personalize your wedding vows and to incorporate other production numbers, feel free to tell your officiating minister these original portions when you meet with him. I'm sure he'll glady include them. In my own wedding my husband fetched me right in the middle of the aisle while the string quartet was serenading us with our theme song. When we stopped at a certain point, our two flower girls danced around us throwing flower petals, eventually releasing live butterflies. Then, my husband and I walked towards the altar where the pastor and my parents were waiting for the "giving away of the bride". You may want to follow the traditional recessional proper. Consult the book of Ms. Bernardo for the Filipino-type and Spanish style wedding march and Ms. Lenderman's book for the traditional religious services. Just a word of warning, finalize with your officiating minister how much time it will take him to finish the entire rites. If you have congregational singing, tell your singers to limit it to 1-2 songs. You don't want your guests to get too hungry or worst bored. Enjoy your wedding ceremony and let your guests enjoy it, too!

Sample Sequence
of the Wedding Ceremony
For A Christian Wedding

I.   Prelude
II. Entourage Song
III. Processional
    A.   Lighting of Candles by the Candle Sponsors
    B.   The Officiating Minister
    C.   The Best Man/Men
    D.   The Groom with his Parents
    E.   The Principal Sponsors
    F.   The Veil Sponsors
    G.   The Cord Sponsors
    H.   The Symbol Bearers
        1. The Bible Bearer
        2. The Ring Bearer
        3. The Coin Bearer
        4. The Ministry Symbol Bearer
    I.   The Groomsmen and the Bridesmaids
    J.   The Junior Groomsmen and the Bridesmaids
    K.   The Flower Girls
    L.   The Matron of Honor and/or the Maid of Honor

     M.   The Bride with her Parents
IV.   Giving Away of the Bride
V.   Scripture Reading
VI.   Opening Prayer
VII.   Congregational Singing (if possible, limit to 2 songs only)
VIII. Exhortation
IX.   Exchange of Marriage Vows
X.   Symbols of Marriage
     A.   Ring and Coin Ceremony
     B.   Bible Presentation
     C.   Veil and Coin Ceremony
     D.   Ministry Symbols
XI.   Communion
XII.   Signing of the Marriage Contract
XIII. Prophetic Prayer of the Pastor and Prayer of Selected Godparents
XIV. Removal of the Veil and Cord
XV.   Lighting of the Unity Candle
XVI. Honoring of Parents
XVII. Benediction
XVIII. Pronouncement
XIX. Pictorial Sequence
XX.   Recessional

There are one and a thousand ways to enjoy your reception. Below is a sample of the reception program. You may want to include production numbers you have in mind (e.g. money tree dance, first dance of the couple, a nephew/niece who will render a song, etc.).

Sample Reception Programme

*Time
Allotment*

  _____ 1. Welcoming of the newlyweds
  _____ 2. Opening prayer (celebration)
  _____ 3. Introduction of the principal sponsors
  _____ 4. Introduction of parents

	5. Opening prayer (food)
_____	6. Dinner feast
_____	7. Video showing (love story) / Well-wishers
_____	8. Tributary toast
_____	9. Cake-cutting & wine toast
_____	10. Kiss the doves / Dove releasing
_____	11. Pull-out favors
_____	12. Bouquet throwing
_____	13. Garter throwing
_____	14. Photo & video session
_____	15. Couple's acknowledgment
_____	16. Signing off by the emcee
_____	17. Opening of gifts

WORD OF ADVICE:

- Formal wedding portrait should be taken as early as possible. In our case, my husband and I had the pictorial session 2 hours before the wedding rites while my make-up was still fresh. In fact, we had a heyday during this photo session, we we're so relaxed and enjoyed every moment of it! If you don't agree with this kind of arrangement because you want your husband to see you the first time in your bridal gown during the march, you can ask your photographer to setup the portrait area near your reception site. Here you can have the pictorials just before the start of the reception.

- You may do away with the reception line if your guests one more than 300. It will eat a lot of your reception time to receive them all and for sure they will be hungry by the time you're done with the receiving line. Otherwise, for a small number of guests, you can personally do the receiving of guests or you can request your parents to receive them while you are having pictorials at the portrait area. Make sure that there is a background music (string quartet/pianist/piped-in) as your guests are entering the reception site.

- Prepare an enlarged floor lay-out and table assigments which you can display just outside the reception area which your guests can refer to for their seating assignments. It is understood that you already informed your guests where they are seated (during the reception) through an insert card that you sent together with your invitation (*"We have placed _____ seat/s for you. You are seated at table no. ___"*). Instead of the enlarged floor lay-out posted, you can also give your ushers a copy of the floor plan and the seating assignments .

- Let ushers lead your guests to their respective seats. Assign an usher to assists the group he's familiar with. For e.g. request a relative of the groom to handle the guests on his side, while somebody from the bride's side can assists her relatives. A college friend can usher your college friends and so on. The usher (though he is not expected to be familiar with all of the guests) should make it easy for the guests to find their respective seats.

  I'd like to say that you should do away with the place cards, except for those in the presidential table and a RESERVED place card for the table/s of your immediate family members and relatives. You don't want your other guests to feel not as important as those guests seated on a table with a place card.

- If you plan to show a video presentation of your love story, limit it to a maximum of 15 minutes. In some instances, the well-wishers were interviewed in advance and this portion is shown as part of the entire video presentation. In the absence of the video showing, the emcee can call a maximum of 3 people who can give their wishes for 2-3 minutes. Make sure they were informed of this task beforehand so they can prepare.

- The toast happens after the dessert has been served. Traditionally, the best man offers the toast to the couple and the groom gives his response. On the other hand, as an alternative to signal the start of the reception, the bride's father and the groom's father may give a short speech each and toast the newlyweds, i.e. if they are amenable to do so.

- The cake-cutting happens after the groom's response to the best man's toast. Ask the single ladies to gather around for the pull-out favors and take advantage of this moment to request them to stay for the bouquet throwing.

- Check with the management of the reception site if doves are allowed to be released from the cage (some hotels are not allowing this - they only allow the 'kiss the dove' style).

- Ask your ushers or bridesmaids to distribute your give-aways while your guests are busy eating dinner. Get a table for the signature frame or guest book and place it to where it is accessible to all. Assign somebody to assist the guests in signing. In lieu of this, message cards/book of memories can be placed on each table (prepare also pens) so guests can write down their names, contact numbers, etc. and personal wishes for the couple. Remind the emcee to announce the message cards/book of memories or the signature frame and guest book.

- There are a lot of creative ways to do the bouquet throwing. The bride may hand it over to a "favorite" single lady whom she wants to "walk down the aisle next", or let the single ladies gather for the traditional throwing of the bouqet. Others want to eliminate the traditional way of doing the garter throwing. Another option is to gather the bachelors to form a circle and ask them to do a limbo rock. Or give each of them balloons and asked them to pop it. One special balloon contains a special saying inside and whoever gets it is the designated partner of the lady who got the bouquet.

Just remember to do these activities without turning your

reception into a children's party.

- You can do away with table hopping. Instead, ask the couple to sit in a comfortable sofa with a nice backdrop then request the guests (per table or group) to join the couple for the pictorials.

What are the things we need to do after the wedding?

"I don't like to overlook anything, so please brief me on the things to do after my big day."

After your big day, do the following:

THINGS TO DO:

- Submit marriage contract within the required fifteen-day period
- Return rented materials and things borrowed
- Dry clean the bridal gown and store it properly
- Keep the wedding accessories (headdress, trains and veils, gloves, shoes, wedding paraphernalias like the Bible, veil and cord, pillows, plum pens, etc.)
- Ask your florist to freeze-dry your bouquet or air dry it yourself
- Keep cake topper and store left-over cake
- Schedule meeting with photographer for picture selection
- Arrange for post-wedding announcement in the newspaper
- Post wedding pictures in the internet
- Arrange post-wedding party for loved ones and close friends
- Send thank-you cards

What are the requirements for the application of the marriage license?

"Though we are just both 18 years of age, we believe with all our hearts that we really love each other and are ready to face the responsibilities of married life.

> *to face the responsibilities of married life. Can you please tell us the requirements in obtaining the marriage license? We would like to save time and effort in all our wedding planning activities since we are both working and studying at the same time."*

Think twice and think hard before you settle down. You are still young and I believe you should not rush into marriage because your emotions are up and high. You mentioned that you are both working students. Why not finish your studies first and get a permanent job to save for your wedding? Your age range still falls into the minor category and need the consent of parents before you settle down.

For purposes of information, the following is the step-by-step guideline being followed in the application of marriage license (comprehensive for all age range) in the Philippines . This is the result of interviews conducted at the Manila and Quezon Civil Registry offices. Unless otherwise specified, the requirements of both municipalities are the same. Ascertain the requirements with your local municipality as there may be slight differences on a case to case basis.[6]

Step 1. Both of the contracting parties must secure their respective birth certificates either from the local municipality where born (Certified True Copy or CTC) or from the National Statistics Office (NSO) as proof of their ages.

In the absence of the birth certificates, the original or CTC of the baptismal certificates can be shown. In the event that it is still not available, the current residence certificate or the sworn declaration of two witnesses who are the nearest of kin of the contracting parties will do, as defined in Article 12 of the New Family Code.[7]

Article 10 reads: "In case either of the contracting parties has been previously married, the applicant shall be required to furnish, instead of the birth or baptismal certificate . . . the death certificate of the deceased spouse or the judicial decree of the absolute divorce, or the judicial decree of annulment or declaration of nullity of his or her previous marriage. In case the death certificate cannot be secured, the party shall make an affidavit setting forth this circumstance and his or her actual civil status and the name and date of death of the deceased spouse."[8]

Step 2. Any one of the parties must prepare any valid ID to show proof that he/she is a resident of the local municipality where they intend to apply for the license. *(Note: The Civil Registry office of Quezon City is accepting the Community Tax Certificate or "cedula" as a valid identification).*

Step 3. Both of the contracting parties must present the document proving their age and the valid identification to the local Civil Registry office to obtain the marriage license application form. There is a fee for filing and the form.
(Note: Fees vary per municipality).

Step 4. Attend the required seminar/s (**family planning** seminar is conducted by the Health Department and/or the **counseling session** taken cared of by DSWD) and get the corresponding certificate/s required. Depending on the age range of the contracting parties, refer to the following for the additional requirements:

Case 1. Minor, age between 18 but below 21 years old. Accomplish Municipal Form No. 92 entitled *Consent to Marriage of a Person Under Age* or simply called *Consent of Parents* form and attend both the family planning and counseling seminars.

Case 2. Age between 21 but below 25 years old. Accomplish Municipal Form No. 7 and 8 entitled *Sworn Statement That Advise of Parents or Guardian Has Been Asked* and *Advise Upon Intended Marriage* respectively or simply called *Parental Advise* form and attend both the family planning and counseling seminars.

Case 3. Age 25 years old and above are required to attend the family planning seminar only. *(Note: If both parties fall on different age range, the other party must be present at the required parental consent or parental advise seminar, e.g., if the female party is only 18 yeas old while the male party is 27 years old, the couple is obligated to attend both seminars).*

Step 5. Submit the duly filled-out marriage license application form, document proving the age and seminar certification/s. *(Note: At the Manila Civil Registry office, the couple is required to attend the oath-taking before the above-mentioned documents are accepted and marriage license is processed).*

Step 6. Wait for eleven (11)* days to get the approved license. *(Note: * - this is the waiting time at the Civil Registry of Quezon City. At the Manila Civil Registry office, the waiting period is 10 days counting from the receipt of the marriage license).*

11

If one of the parties is a foreigner, what are the requirements for the marriage license?

"My fiancee is an American citizen and we decided to get married here in the Philippines. How should we go about obtaining the marriage license?"

Your fiancé must obtain the *Certificate of Legal Capacity to Marry* from his embassy, a copy of the divorce papers (if applicable) and a photocopy of his passport.[9] Together with your authenticated birth certificate and valid ID, you are now ready to proceed to your local civil registry to apply for the license (see item no. 10 as guide).

12

What are the formal requisites of marriage in the Philippines?

"I already have the marriage license. Will this suffice for a valid marriage?"

It's a good thing that you asked. Many couples due to their excitement and haste to enter into marriage, realized too late that they entered into invalid marriage in the absence of the following legal requirements:

"Under the New Family code, the marrying age is 18 years old and above. . . . If any of the parties is below 18 years of age, the marriage is void even if the consent of the parents has been previously obtained."[10]   The formal requisites of marriage in the Philippines as provided for in Article 2 of the New Family Code reads:

(1) "Authority of the solemnizing officer
(2) A valid marriage license . . .[except in the case of marriage of exceptional character]

(3) A marriage ceremony which takes place with the
appearance of the contracting parties before the
solemnizing officer and their personal declaration that
they take each other husband and wife in the presence
of not less than two witnesses of legal age." [11]

The absence of any one of these legal requirements will result
to an illegitimate marriage and illegitimate children as well. "…there
can be no proxy marriages here like in California."[12] Make sure
that you satisfy not only one but all the other legal requirements.

Marriages **between Filipino citizens abroad** is valid as long as
the legal requirements are met. According to Article 10 of the New
Family Code: "Marriages between Filipino citizens abroad may be
solemnized by a consul-general, consul or vice-consul of the Republic of the Philippines. The issuance of the marriage license and
the duties of the local civil registrar and of the solemnizing officer
with regard to the celebration of marriage shall be performed by
said consular official."[13] Since their authority to solemnize marriage abroad is limited to Filipino citizens only, a marriage between
a Filipino and foreigner abroad solemnized by a Philippine consul
appears to be void.[14] "However, by way of exception, if the marriage
between the foreigner and the Filipino citizen abroad solemnized
by a Philippine consul assigned in that country is recognized as
valid in the host country, then such marriage shall be considered
valid in the Philippines."[15]

13

How does the marriage license and
marriage contract/certificate differ?

*"I got the shock of my life during the day
of my wedding when I found out that it
was not a marriage contract /certificate
that was prepared but a marriage license.
It was a good thing I was able to check on
it before the wedding ceremony started.*

> *It seems that many were confused on the difference of the two. Please explain how these two differ so this inadvertent error will not be repeated anymore in the future."*

The following discussion distinguishes the marriage license from the marriage certificate/contract:[16]

The **marriage license** *(Municipal Form No. 90)* is the document issued to the couple prior to marriage by the Civil Registry office of the local municipality upon fulfillment of specific requirements. Under Philippine laws, the marriage license legally allows the couple to marry anywhere in the Philippines within the 120-day period counting from the date of scheduled issuance (indicated at the right top most part of the form). After 120 days the license will expire; that is, if the marriage did not take place within the said time frame for some reason or another, the couple will have to reapply for another marriage license before they can get married.

The **certificate of marriage** *(Municipal Form No. 97)* which is also known as the **marriage contract** is the document signed in quadruplicate by the couple, solemnizing officer and the principal witnesses ("ninongs" and "ninangs") during the actual wedding ceremony. The duly completed typewritten contract is filed with the municipality (Civil Registry of Marriage) which has jurisdiction over the church/place of marriage. The couple will get their copy of the contract after the Civil Registry processes it.

"The marriage certificate is not a requirement for a valid marriage. Hence even if you did not sign a written marriage contract or certificate after the marriage ceremony, there is still a valid marriage if all the legal requirements . . . are present. A written marriage contract is merely an evidence of marriage."[17] A marriage with a completely signed marriage contract but without a valid marriage license is null and void except for cases like the marriage of exceptional character[18] *(please refer to item no. 21).*

What is the purpose of the waiting period before the marriage license is released?

> *"My fiancé is a seaman and was given a vacation of few weeks within which we intend to tie the knot. When we filed the marriage license application form in Quezon City, we were informed that we have to wait for another eleven (11) days before the release of the marriage license. I'm just wondering why it has to take this long just to get it?"*

The waiting period before the release of the marriage license is not a waste of time but vital for the following reasons: [19]

Immediately the next day after the submission of the duly filled-up marriage license application form, a form called the **Notice** (*Municipal Form No. 94)* is posted by the City Civil Registry for ten (10) consecutive days on a bulletin board near the main door of its office for the purpose of informing the public of a couple's intent to marry. The waiting period is a safety tool against hocus-pocus because any reported opposition or knowledge of any legal impediment to such marriage will cause non-issuance of the license to marry.

It pays to wait so you know you're safe.

Who prepares the marriage contract and who submits it?

> *"I'd like to know who prepares the marriage certificate/contract and who is responsible to submit it."*

The marriage certificate or contract is prepared and processed in the following manner:[20]

The church or the solemnizing officer's office prepares the *Certificate of Marriage* in quadruplicate. Only the first copy is originally typewritten while the rest are just carbon copies. This is to ensure that there will be no changing /editing of information on the remaining pages.

The certificate of marriage must be submitted within the next fifteen (15) days counting from the date of marriage to the municipality which has jurisdiction over the wedding ceremony's venue. The church's staff, the secretary of the officiating minister, any trusted person or even the couple themselves can submit the marriage contract. All copies of the marriage contract are submitted to the local Civil Registry for processing (upon payment of filing fee). The registry number is written on the form. Two copies remain to the Civil Registry (one copy is for the Civil Registry and the OCRG copy is sent to NSO), the third copy is for the solemnizing officer and the original copy is for the couple.

16 What is the use of SECPA and the CTC copies of the marriage certificate/contract?

> *"I just got married and I want to renew my passport to reflect my new surname. I was told that I need a SECPA copy of my marriage contract for passport renewal. Why can't I use a CTC copy?"*

The acquisition of SECPA or CTC copies of the marriage certificate/contract follows the procedure listed below:[21]

A security paper or SECPA copy of the marriage contract is one of the vital requirements in the application of a passport or visa and for all other local requirements. It is normally available at NSO 4-6 months after the marriage certificate/contract is filed. If the SECPA copy is immediately requested in Manila, the transmittal form is obtained from the Civil Registry office and submitted with NSO.

The SECPA copy is readily available in Quezon City civil registry office, and only submitted with NSO for authentication. A Certified True Copy (CTC) is available at the local municipality after one to three days upon submission of the marriage contract/certificate and valid only for local use.

What happens when the contract/certificate of marriage is not submitted on time?

> *"After our 2-week honeymoon, my husband and I went to the local Civil Registry office to submit our marriage contract. However, we found out that we were late in submission. Is there a penalty for this?"*

The paper requirements for delayed submission of marriage certificate/contract can be gleaned in the following discussion:[22]

At the Quezon City Civil Registry office, delayed registration of certificate of marriage necessitates an affidavit explaining for the late registration, a copy of the marriage contract and a filing fee.

At the City Civil Registry of Manila, aside from the usual filing fee the complete requirements for delayed registration are listed below:
1. Census - negative result
2. No Record - City Civil Registry (CCR)
3. Affidavit of solemnizing officer/ authority of solemnizing officer (NSO)
4. Affidavit of contracting parties and birth certificate of children
5. Affidavit of two witnesses
6. Preparation of marriage contract -revised form
7. Original marriage contract

It is still best to submit the marriage contract within the fifteen

(15)-day period counting from the date of marriage so as not to be burdened with a lot of additional requirements for late submission. For a couple who submitted it after a long period of time and the wife already gave birth, the birth certificate of the baby will be an additional proof of union.

18 What are the other requirements if the wedding ceremony is not held inside the church?

"My fiancé and I decided to get married in a garden wedding setup. Are there other requirements to prepare for this kind of wedding?"

When the marriage ceremony is not held inside the church, the local Civil Registry office requires this additional document attached to the marriage contract/certificate when filed. [23]

A letter of request is prepared addressed to the officiating minister requesting him to solemnize the marriage outside the church, indicating the venue, time and type of wedding (e.g. garden wedding, beach wedding, etc.) The letter is signed by the couple and noted by the officiating minister. Then it is notarized and submitted together with the duly filled-up marriage certificate/contract to the local Civil Registry.

19 Is there such a thing as secret marriage (SM)?

"My friend told me that she and her boyfriend had a secret marriage. Is this legal?"

Secret marriage is defined as follows:[24]

There is no such thing as "secret marriage". The word "secret" was probably coined because the couple did not want their parents (or guardians) to learn of their planned marriage. This "hurried" marriage is actually a civil wedding where a judge officiated the ceremony. This wedding is valid under the law and also requires a marriage license.

20 What about tying the knot with a prisoner?

> "I met my boyfriend in the prisons. Despite the situation, we are serious in tying the knot before the year ends. Can you advise us on what to do?"

When tying a know with a prisoner, the Civil Registry says: [25]
You can still get married but there are restrictions and inconveniences. For instance, the solemnizing officer and couple of witnesses will be there at the prison cell to conduct the ceremony. Your honeymoon will be confined to the prison cell or at a certain place agreed upon with the prison managers. A marriage license is also required.

21 What is a marriage of exceptional character?

> "I've seen in the movies marriages conducted while the other party is dying. Is this true in real life?"

Marriage of exceptional character is really exceptional because it is valid without the presentation of a marriage license. The discussion below answers your question:[26]

Yes, marriages performed while the other contracting party is at the point of death can happen in real life. This is one of the cases in a category called marriage of exceptional character where the marriage license is not required prior to marriage. "In case of a marriage in *articulo mortis*, when the party at the point of death is unable to sign the marriage certificate, it shall be sufficient for one of the witnesses to the marriage to write the name of said party, which fact shall be attested by the solemnizing officer."[27] Included under this category are the ff.: (1) marriages among Muslims or other members of the ethnic cultural communities (e.g. marriages among the Bogobo tribe) (2) the location of one or both of the contracting parties is so located that it is impossible for them to appear personally before the civil registrar, (3) there is no civil registrar in the municipality and (4) situations where there is military conflict . The marriage of couple who has been living together for the last five years can also qualify as a marriage of exceptional character provided there is no legal impediment to marry each other. There is no need to obtain a marriage license to have their marriage solemnized either through church or civil wedding. Only an affidavit is executed to attest that they have been living together for the last five years. The marriage certificate/contract is due for submission within the next thirty days.

22 What about mass weddings?

"I have heard of mass weddings conducted yearly in our community. Please explain this kind of setup."

Mass weddings is a valid wedding and its setup is as follows:[28]

Mass weddings are sponsored by politicians, Rotarians, NGO's or sometimes a religious group or charitable institutions. It is conducted to give couples a chance to tie the knot even though they have very limited budget. Usually, the sponsoring group is the one who arranges the license and chooses the "ninongs" and "ninangs" (sponsor) of the couple.

23 Should we have a wedding rehearsal?

"My wedding day will be three weeks from now. A friend suggested that we should have a wedding rehearsal. How important is a wedding rehearsal?"

A wedding rehearsal is the perfect time for the couple, their wedding party and their spouses or dates, including the parents of the couple, grandparents, and usually key players of the wedding "team" like the soloist and organist to meet and practise. Camaraderie and rapport is not only built but everybody is also briefed of their duties and responsibilities. The line-up of the recessional is arranged and rehearsed (normally with the accompanying music) to make sure that everything will go smoothly on the wedding day itself. If there is a wedding coordinator, he is the one who arranges the line-up of the processional and help with spacing and pace as participants walk down the aisle. The children who are part of the bridal entourage are also encouraged to attend with their parents. The rehearsal will also familiarize the wedding party with the location of the rites to avoid being late on the wedding day itself which delays the ceremony.

The couple should bring food (something to nibble) and drinks for those who will attend the rehearsal. Ideally, it is recommended that the practise be conducted a week before the big day possibly mimicking the time and date of the day of the ceremony.

In Western culture, the rehearsal dinner customarily follows the wedding rehearsal. However, the rehearsal dinner can also be conducted prior to the wedding rehearsal or can be set at some other days.[29] The family of the groom traditionally do the honors of hosting it.

What about additional wedding TIPS?

"I would appreciate if you can give me tips in making my wedding stick to proper decorum."

a. *How do we inform our guests that we prefer cash gifts instead of presents?*

Word of mouth is still the most acceptable way. You can tell your mom to tell your relatives your preference. You can let your relatives tell your preference to the other guests who asked. You can let your relatives tell your preference if they are asked. Do not forget to send thank-you cards to acknowledge every gift gracefully. For cash gifts, let the giver know how you intend to spend their gift.

If you would like to inform the guests in a subtle way that you don't need presents because you are going to reside abroad after the wedding, include a card in your invitation saying:

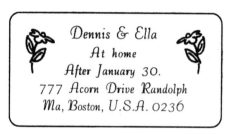

Dennis & Ella
At home
After January 30.
777 *Acorn Drive Randolph*
Ma, Boston, U.S.A. 0236

b. Is it proper to enclose bridal registry cards in the invitation?

Never enclose bridal registry cards in your invitation.
It is not proper that you insinuate that gifts are required if they attend the wedding. Just be thankful if they give you a gift or not. Bring out the registry cards only if somebody asks for it.

c. How important is an R.S.V.P.?

R.S.V.P (can also be written as R.s.v.p.) or *Répondez S'il Vous Plaît* is a French word which means "please respond" or "please answer". As a rule, after the word R.S.V.P., there is a phone number and the name of the contact person whom guests can call to confirm or decline their attendance. It is ethical and very important to respond to an R.S.V.P. so that the couple or the host of a party may know in advance the number of guests who will actually attend the event.

d. What about dress decorum?

Your male entourage wearing "*barong*" is advised never to wear boutonniere because this will destroy the "*barong's*" delicate fabric. If the groom wears a "*barong*" like the rest of your entourage, you can make him wear a garland of an exquisite but simple piece of flower to distinguish him from the rest. Wear a white *camisa-de-chino* underneath the "barong", never a sleeveless, striped or colored and printed undershirt.

Only the male entourage wearing tuxedo or a coat and tie should wear boutonniere on the left lapel, never with a pocket square (pocket squares are placed in the left breast pocket). The groom should wear a flower on the left lapel which is different in color or type to distinguish his place of honor with the rest of the male entourage.

25 What are some of the common wedding customs?

> "Can you discuss the different customs of different nationalities in their wedding preparations?"

According to the "*The Concise Oxford Dictionary*" **custom** refers to the usual way of behaving or acting.[30] It is a particular established way of behaving. The following discussion will enlighten us on the standard engagement and wedding customs and few general practices in selected countries, most of which is taken from *Customs and*

Keepsakes by the editors of the Bride's magazine:[31]

THE RING. When a man gives a *"betrothal"* or engagement ring to a woman, it goes to say that he is ready to ask for her hand in marriage. The engagement ring seals the betrothal and is customarily made of something of high value - usually a diamond stone or other symbolic gemstones like amethyst (luck), emerald (youth), ruby (safety), etc.

The diamond stone became a standard and a popular choice for engagement rings since the fifteenth-century monarchs discovered its enduring qualities. They equated its quality of hardness to an enduring kind of love while they believed its unique sparkle arose from the flames of love.[32] Back in 1477, the first recorded account of a diamond ring offered to seal the engagement vow happened when Maximilian I, King of Germany proposed to Mary of Burgundy.[33]

In the US and other parts of the world, the engagement and wedding rings are sold as a set. The engagement ring carries the gemstone while the plain gold bands are still the most popular for wedding rings (silver and platinum are increasingly becoming popular along with other innovative designs). This follows the rationale that the lady to whom the man will give the engagement ring is the same person he will marry. The circular shape of the ring denotes unending love, suggestive of the geometrical contour of the one and only one shape which has no end.

The English-speaking cultures wear the wedding ring on the ring finger of the left hand owing to the ancient's people belief that this finger is said to have the only vein that runs directly to the heart.[34] For many of the European countries, the wedding ring is worn on the ring finger of the right hand. The Greek woman wears her engagement ring on her left hand, and moves it to the right hand when she gets married. In Germany, even while still engaged, couples are already referred to as bride and bridegroom and give each other gold bands as engagement rings. The rings are worn on the left hand.

THE HUPPAH or CHUPPAH. A *huppah* (sometimes spelled as *chuppah*) is traditionally part of Jewish weddings. It is a canopy embellished with fresh flowers, a hand-painted or embroidered cloth where the couple, the rabbi and cantor stand next to a small table covered in white, set with one or two goblets for ritual wine. The parents and the entire wedding party stand under or near the *huppah* throughout the ceremony. The *huppah* symbolizes three things for the Jews: ancient bridal chamber of consummation, the shelter they used during the nomadic times and the home the newlyweds will share.

THE BRIDAL GOWN. Before Queen Victoria introduced the idea of an all-white gown in 1840, the bride used to wear her best dress of whatever color. White was a symbol of affluence at that time because a white dress would just be used for a few couple of times and soon will be considered soiled. In Roman times, white is a symbol of joy and celebration. At the beginning of the twentieth century, white became synonymous with virginal purity.

However, different cultures wear bridal gowns in different styles and in various colors for some purposes. Chinese brides wear brilliant red gown, signifying joy and love. In India and Nepal, brides put gold dust on their skin and wear gold-threaded *sarees* (cloth of cotton or silk material draped round the body). Japanese brides change clothes many times during their weddings. It can be from the traditional white wedding kimonos to Western-style wedding gowns, then at the reception, colorful kimonos and ball gowns in the bride's favorite color. In the West, bridal gowns are styled differently and made in variety of hues to match the discriminating taste of the bride. The gown reflects the bride's personality and set the style of the wedding. The bride chooses a gown that will not just flatter her figure but one which is within her budget.

THE VEIL. When Rebekah was about to meet the young Isaac, she took the veil and covered herself (Genesis 24:65). In the East during those times, as a sign of modesty for a young unmarried woman, she appropriately covers herself with a veil when she is about to come into the company of a man. Thus, the veil conveyed youth and virginity. In the sixteenth century, the veil was chosen for adornment.

THE WEDDING FLOWERS. There is not a wedding without flowers. Because flowers bring such a special feeling and warmth to the heart, they has been synonymous to happiness and love during weddings. The various types of wedding flowers and their colors stir emotions and bring many symbolical merits. There are cases where couples splurge the most on flowers because they wish to create an ambiance of gaiety and celebration on their big day. In Hawaii, both the Bride and the Groom have leis while in India, the couple wear floral headdress.

THE KISS. The *kiss* from early Roman times was a legal bond that sealed contracts. The *kiss* is permitted at the end of the rites to announce a new status. When the couple kissed, it was believed that a part of their souls was left behind in the other as their breath was exchanged. In the Bible, *kiss* means either intimacy or betrayal. When one *kisses* somebody in an intimate way, he/she must be sure that he's/she's really in-love and mean it. Therefore an insincere kiss is a form of betrayal.

THE CAKE. The wedding cake whether small or big, simple or intricately designed is always present during the wedding reception. The cake has been a symbol of fertility and good fortune. It is designed to match the wedding style incorporating the color motif and theme. The cake topper maybe any kind of decoration ranging from the traditional bride and groom figurines to the fancy figurines which display the couple's interest and hobbies or just something like fresh flowers.

In the Western culture, there is such a thing as a second cake. Called the groom's cake which is traditionally a dark fruitcake (but can also be a chocolate cake) to contrast the lightly-colored wedding cake., it can have a shape that conforms to the interest of the groom (e.g. basketball, skii, etc).[35] The groom's cake serves as a second dessert but traditionally are given to guests as take home - sliced and placed in a decorated box. According to customs, the couple share their wedding cake or the groom's cake to guests to impart the same good fortune and sweetness of the married life.

THE WEDDING FAVORS. During the reception, the guests receive mementos of the wedding, a way by which the couple say their thank-you for sharing their special day. Since the couple are considered blessed including anything they touched, the favors or commonly called give-aways will serve as tokens that will bring the same kind of good fortune and blessings to the guests.

THE HONEYMOON. Ancient marriages by capture occur when a man would literally "capture" the woman he likes (many times against her will!) and put her into hiding for a month from searching relatives and friends. For thirty days (one full moon to another full moon), the couple drink a fermented honey drink, known as *mead* or *metheglin*, thus "honeymoon". Honey is known to be an ancient symbol of life, health and fertility and this concoction may have eased sexual inhibitions. This "month-long" sweetness or "honeymoon" is a time of escape before facing the realities of marriage responsibilities.

26 What are the other ways to get married?

"Kindly give me ideas that will help me conceptualize my dream wedding, unique and original on its own."

About 75% of all marriages take place in some form of religious establishment.[36] However, the new generation of audacious couple wanting to get married, whose needs and wishes need to be satisfactorily met caused the emergence of the many ways on how to conduct the wedding celebration, whether inside or outside the religious establishment. Conforming to the couple's needs and wants, together reflecting their heritage, personal tastes, style and statement, below are various ways by which couples can celebrate - and celebrate in style the most awaited occasion of their lives. (Source: *Bride's New Ways to Wed: A Guide to Personalizing Your Wedding* by the editors of *Bride's* magazine and *Bride's All New Book of Etiquette*).

a. **Theme weddings.** Weddings with a theme.

1. The theme may be a season of the year.
   Weddings of this sort take place near a certain holiday or a certain season of the year. These weddings may have any of the following holidays as a theme: Christmas, Valentine, Fourth of July, Halloween, Thanksgiving, New Year's Eve or New Year's Day. The atmosphere brings added fun, and décor during seasons like Christmas will just be additions.

2. Outdoor or garden theme.
   Outdoor or garden weddings is appropriate during spring or summer and in the Philippines, during dry months (though the weather is really very unpredictable). This is the most risky and should have an alternative plan in case the weather does not cooperate (e.g. use of tents or transfer to an indoor facility in case of a heavy downpour).

3. The theme may be a period or era.

   The Renaissance/Medieval , Victorian, Edwardian period's costumes and décor add to the flair.

4. Military theme.
   Both or one of the couple is a military person. It is a dramatic way to honor military status with a beautiful celebration. The style of the wedding is dictated by "tradition" rather than strict laws.

5. Ethnic weddings.

This wedding incorporates the traditions and customs of the couple's background with traditional costumes, music, food, etc.

The theme may vary and may include sports as a theme, or a nautical one. Just be creative and think of ways by which you can show your guests your common interests, hobbies and other things which both of you would want to showcase on your wedding — a theme which will be your statement personified.

b. **Weekend weddings.** Weekend wedding is a 2-3 days wedding celebration (may start from Friday evening till Sunday afternoon) that offers your guests additional activities throughout the weekend beyond the normal wedding festivities. There may be a wedding/dinner rehearsal and a day of pre-planned activities (team sports, picnicking or pool party, sightseeing). The highlight and the central event is of course the wedding and reception. The fun-filled activities are prepared to help guests unwind and have a mini-vacation, meet new friends, and give a chance to the two families to build camaraderie and rapport.

c. **Progressive Wedding.** The bride and groom and their close relatives and friends take the celebration on the road, traveling to predetermined spots, such as his and her hometowns—for reception and parties hosted in the newlywed's honor. This works for couple with large groups of friends and family scattered in different locations or with divorced parents who are not able to attend the wedding.

d. **Destination Wedding.** Similar to weekend wedding in format and principle, but the location you choose for the wedding is the place where you want to take a vacation. This is sometimes referred to as a travel wedding because you travel to the location or honeymoon wedding. The destination serves as the honeymoon spot (tropical island or state park). The honeymoon wedding is suitable for couples who have children from prior marriages, because it allows the two merging families to spend time together. Popular spots are Disney World in Florida, Disneyland in California, Hawaii and Las Vegas. A cruise ship can be an attractive spot for your destination wedding. The guests are responsible for their own air fares and hotel costs.

(Engaged)

(Married)

Ernesto & Nelia
De Guzman
have been happily married
since April, 2001

Pastor Dante officiating Ernie & Nel's wedding.

❧Conclusion

A friend wrote an original composition, entitled, *"True Love Comes from God"*. How true this is! The only way a relationship can last until death is when love emanates from the heart of God. Therefore, if you, our readers, are able to receive the message we are trying to convey in this book, it is putting God in the center of your love life. If you are in the process of looking for a partner, ask God. He is the giver of every good and perfect gift. If you are engaged, seek to honor Him in your relationship. If you just got married, make God your partner. From the following passage of the Scriptures we will find the key to a lifetime treasure in relationship. The Psalmist confirms the conclusion of all the researches and studies about keeping the family relationship truly blessed; that it all begins with establishing the fear of the Lord in our hearts.

THE KEY TO A BLESSED FAMILY

Psalm 128:1 – 6

Blessed are all who fear the
Lord,
who walk in His ways.
You will eat the fruit of your
labor;
Blessings and prosperity
will be yours.
Your wife will be like a fruitful
vine

within your house;
Your sons will be like olive
shoots
around your table.
Thus is the man blessed
who fears the Lord.
May the Lord bless you from
Zion
all the days of your life;
May you see the prosperity of
Jerusalem,
and may you live to see your
children's children.
Peace be upon Israel..

Below is a poignant story of true love. This was lifted from the book, *I LOVE YOU* by Gordon O. Martinborough (used with permission).

"*It was a January 16, 1935, and on the beautiful Caribbean Island of Barbados, a baby was born and was named Timothy. As he matured, this brilliant youth traveled to the neighboring island of Trinidad where he studied at Caribbean Union College. There he met a special Guyanese girl named Thelda. Gradually a bond of affection and love drew their lives together.*

Tim's goal was to become a physician, and soon he migrated to the United States of America. But in his second year of medical school, tragedy struck! On that awful night of May 16, 1959, a reckless vehicle knocked his car off.

His cervical spine was broken and he was paralyzed from the neck down. Without the use of his arms and legs, he would be a quadriplegic for the rest of his life. Over the next 10 months of rehabilitation, Tim was taught to operate a motorized wheelchair. He also learned the use of a device which gave him limited movement to his thumb, middle finger and forefinger so he could write and handle his own telephone.

Tim made up his mind that he would still become a doctor, if the University will accept him. Despite the limitations of his body, he would use his brain. He had faith in God, in himself, and he drew upon the faith of his family, his father being a gospel minister while his mother cradled him a second time.

The University decided to permit him to continue. Tim arrived on the campus with his wheelchair,. He had to conquer the physical challenges of moving from one classroom to another, the social pressures of interacting with people, some of whom were not so helpful. He persevered and graduated on June 3, 1963 receiving a standing ovation! For the next four years he pursued a specialty in pathology and is now director of Cytology, and associate professor of Pathology at the Medical Center of Southern California, Los Angeles.

Meanwhile, Thelda also migrated to the U.S. and completed her training as a nurse in Illinois. She was sure that because of Timothy's handicap, she could not marry him, although deep inside, she still loved him. She felt an obligation to honor the promise she had made to him before the accident. She was convinced that her conscience would not allow her to be happy if she deserted him to marry someone else.

In 1969, some 10 years after the accident, this couple met for the first time. It was an encounter charged with many conflicting emotions. During the 70's Thelda did orthopaedic nursing and mastered the ability to deal with the handicapped. But more than that she met patients who had spouses. While some of them married before their tragedy, she observed that some still enjoyed a marital encounter. She came to a decision that if Tim proposed to her, she would marry

A decade has come and gone, and their love still lives on. Their devotion is a perpetual inspiration.

him. As the currents of love swept over their hearts, Tim gathered enough strength to ask. They were engaged in 1980 and were married a year after.

A decade has come and gone, and their love still lives on. Their devotion is a perpetual inspiration. Recently, I spoke with them again. As Tim told of his love and Thelda spoke of hers, I noted the word, "Tim is a special person, and I feel no embarrassment, whatever, in public when he sits in wheelchair and I stand by his side. I have always been faithful to him and I ever will be."

This is a beautiful story of love in spite of. This is possible because this is the same love that comes from the heart of God who is love. We pray that this story has inspired you more to pursue and seek for such love that comes only from God.

OUR PRAYER

"Lord, it is our earnest desire that the reader will know You the way You want to be known, a Holy, loving God. That he will come to know you as his Lord and Savior, thus allow You to rule and reign in his heart. It is only in this way Lord, that he will have the fear of You, which is the very foundation of how to keep himself pure and holy. That You will be the center of his love life. That he will seek to know Your will and obey it. In Jesus' name. Amen."

YOUR PRAYER

"Lord Jesus, I realize my sinfulness and shortcomings. I am truly sorry. Please forgive me and remove my guilt. Thank you for your blood that cleanses me. I ask You to come into my heart and be my Savior and Lord. Please help me to change and to obey Your will."

If you responded to this prayer and allowed the Lord Jesus to come into your heart to be your Lord and Savior, you are now a born again child of God. Being born again establishes your new position as a child of God. Anyone who is joined to Christ is a new person. The old sinful nature is gone; the new nature has come (John 1:12; 2 Corinthians 5:17). Therefore, you are no longer under the rulership of satan but of Christ. It is not a matter of changing your religion nor attending church regularly but of establishing a genuine relationship with Christ. It is an experience with God. A divine relationship is established when you confess sincerely from your heart Jesus Christ to be the Lord and Savior of your life. The fear of God is now planted in your heart to guide you to walk in the ways of God. You will begin to hunger and thirst for the things of God like bible reading, praying and worshipping God in a different manner. You will begin to love others as God loved you and gave His life for you. You will long to have fellowship with those who have the same experience with God that and you will study the Bible, pray and worship God with them.

❦Endnotes

Chapter 1
LOVE

[1] David B. Duralnik, ed.-in-chief, *Webster's New World Dictionary* (Ohio: William Collins Publishers, 1980) 838.

[2] Evelyn Miranda-Feliciano, *Love and Courtship, 3rd ed.* (Metro Manila, Philippines: OMF Literature, Inc., 1997)16.

[3] Aglow Magazine.

[4] Gene Parado, *Of Love and Lovers* (Metro Manila, Philippines: Cacho Hermanos, 1985)12-17.

[5] Ray E. Short, *Sex, Love or Infatuation* (Quezon City, Philippines: Imprint of Claretian Publications, 1998) 53-54.

[6] Aglow Magazine.

[7] Short 22.

[8] Feliciano 20.

Chapter 2
SEX

[1] *Webster's New World Dictionary* 1305.

[2] Romeo R. Ticzon, *Sex Education 1* (Philippines: Romeo R. Ticzon Publisher, 1993) 17.

[3] Ticzon 17.

[4] Joshua Harris, *Boy Meets Girl.* (USA: Multnomah Publishers, Inc., 2001)157-158.

[5] Ticzon 17.

[6] Dr. Isabelo Magalit. *Why Wait Till Marriage?* (Philippines: OMF Literature, Inc., 1992) 3-4.

[7] Ticzon 17.

[8] Short 97-105.

⁹ Carlo M. Magdaluyo, "Sex in the Christian Family", *Aglow Magazine* 24 Apr. 1989: 8
¹⁰ Ticzon 17.
¹¹ Ticzon 17.

Chapter 4
BLESSED SINGLENESS

¹ Dante and Cynthia Veluz, *Hear & Obey* (Quezon City, Philippines: Jesus, the Heart of Missions, Inc.,1999) 187.

Chapter 5
COURTSHIP

¹ *Webster's New World Dictionary* 326.
² quoted from Bong Baylon, *Aglow Magazine* (cut out from magazine, no date).

Chapter 6
ENGAGEMENT

¹ Miriam Webster, *Webster's New Students Dictionary* (New York: American Book Company, 1964) 278.
² Feliciano 102.

Chapter 7
WEDDING PREPARATIONS

¹ Conchitina Sevilla-Bernardo, *The Compleat Filipino* (Pasig City, Philippines: Anvil Publishing, Inc., 1997) 237.
² Bride's Maids & Co., *Veil - An Annual* Guidebook (Pasig City, Philippines: BRIDE'S MAIDS, 1999) 57.
³ Bride's Maids & Co. 57.
⁴ Teddy Lenderman, *The Complete Idiot's Guide to The Perfect Wedding* (New York: Macmillan, 1997) 153 .
⁵ Bride's Magazine editors, *Bride's All New Book of Etiquette* (New York: Putnam, 1993) 34.

[6] Conrado Nunez, Jr., Carmelita Dela Cruz and Bombita, Estella, personal interview. October 2001.

[7] The New Family Code 500.

[8] The New Family Code 499.

[9] Personal interview.

[10] Bride's Maids & Co. 42.

[11] The New Family Code 497.

[12] Bride's Maids & Co. 42.

[13] The New Family Code 499.

[14] Melencio S. Sta. Maria, Jr., *Persons and Family Relations Law*, 3rd ed., (Quezon City, Philippines: Rex Bookstore, 1999) 132.

[15] Sta. Maria 132.

[16] Personal interview.

[17] Bride's Maids & Co. 42.

[18] Bride's Maids & Co. 42.

[19] Personal interview.

[20] Personal interview.

[21] Personal interview.

[22] Personal interview.

[23] Personal interview.

[24] Personal interview.

[25] Personal interview.

[26] Personal interview.

[27] The New Family Code 498.

[28] Personal interview.

[29] Lenderman 65.

[30] Della, Thomson, ed. *The Concise Oxford Dictionary,* 9th ed., (New York: Oxford University Press, 1995) 332.

[31] Bride's Magazine editors, *Bride's Little Book of Customs and Keepsakes* (New York: Clarkson Potter, 1994) 12-45.

[32] Lenderman 5.

[33] Bride's All New Book 11.

[34] Bride's All New Book 11.

[35] Lenderman 212.

[36] Lenderman 217.

❧Bibliography

Baylon, Bong, Carlo Magdaluyo and Harold Sala. *Aglow Magazine.* Philippines 1988-1989 edition.

Bernardo, Conchitina. *The Compleat Filipino.* Pasig City, Philippines: Anvil Publishing, Inc., 1997.

Bride's Maids & Co. *Veil - an Annual Guidebook Vol. 1.* Pasig City: Philippines, 1999.

Duralnik, David B., ed. in-chief. *Webster's New World Dictionary.* Ohio: William Collens, 1980.

Editors of BRIDE'S magazine. *Bride's Little Book of Customs and Keepsakes.* New York: Clarkson N. Potter, 1994.

Editors of BRIDE's magazine. *Bride's All New Book of Etiquette.* New York: Putnam, 1993.

Editors of Bride's magazine with Antonia Vander Meer. *Bride's New Ways to Wed - a Guide to Personalizing your Wedding.* New York: Berkley, 1990.

Feliciano, Evelyn. *Love and Courtship.* 3rd ed. Mandaluyong, Philippines: OMF Literature, Inc., 1999.

Harris, Joshua. *Boy Meets Girl.* USA: Multomah, 2001.

Lenderman, Teddy. *The Complete Idiot's Guide to the Perfect Wedding,* 2nd ed. New York: Macmillan, 1991.

Magalit, Isabelo F. *Why Wait Till Marriage?* Mandaluyong, Philippines:OMF Literature, Inc., 1997.

Neri, Rita. *The Essentials of Wedding Workbook.* Manila: Anvil Publishing Inc., 1998.

Nunez, Conrado Jr., Carmelita Dela Cruz and Estella Bombita. Personal interview. October 2001.

Parado, Gene. *Of Love & Lovers.* Philippines: Cacho Hermanos, 1985.

Philippines. *The New Family Code.* Manila, Philippines: Rex Bookstore, 1999.

Post, Peggy. *Emily Post's Wedding Planner.* 3rd ed. New York: HarperCollins, 1999.

Short, Ray E. *Sex, Love or Infatuation*. Philippines: Claretian Publications, 1998.

Sta. Maria, Melencio S. Jr., *Persons and Family Relations Law*, 3rd ed. Quezon City, Philippines: Rex Bookstore, 1999.

Stewart, Martha. *The Best of Martha Stewart Living Weddings*. New York: Clarkson Potter, 1999.

Thompson, Della, ed. *The Concise Oxford Dictionary*, 9th ed. New York, Oxford U P, 1995.

Ticzon, Romeo R. *Sex Education Manual I & II*. Philippines: Romeo Ticzon, 1993.

Veluz, Dante and Cynthia. *Hear & Obey*. Quezon City, Philippines: Jesus the Heart of Missions Team, 1999.

Webster, Miriam. *Webster's New Student's Dictionary*. New York: American Book Company, 1964.

🌹 About The Authors

Dr. Dante and Cynthia Veluz are the founders and International Directors of Jesus, the Heart of Missions Team, Inc. (Philippines). They are also the Directors of the JHMT Ministry Academy. Dr. Dante is the President, while Rev. Cynthia is the Vice President for Operations of the JHMT Bible College.

Dr. Dante is a graduate of A.B. Political Science at the Lyceum of the Philippines and Central Bible College (CBC) in Manila. He served as faculty member of CBC (5 years) and Foursquare Bible College (2 years). He was the founder and former chapter president of Born-Again Christian Fellowship (BACF), a campus ministry of the Inter-Varsity Christian Fellowship (IVCF). Prior to entering the ministry, he was the chairman and president of HIS Realty and Construction Development Company.

Rev. Cynthia earned the degree of Bachelor of Science in Chemistry at Adamson University in Manila and became part of its faculty for 5 years. She studied at the Central Bible College where she headed various church ministries such as Sunday School, Christian Education Board, Youth and Church camps and the Professional's Group. She was the former general manager of Dunkin Donuts' Mix Plant prior to entering the ministry.

The couple also hosts a regular radio program, LOVELIFE at DWSS, 1494 Khz AM Band (Philippines). Aside from Lovelife, they are also authors of Hear & Obey Book (1998) and co-authors & General Editor of the Signs & Wonders Book (1999). They serve as directors of the Hear & Obey Conferences, Lovelife Specials Seminars and Women on Fire Conferences conducting revival & love, courtship and marriage seminars since 1992, in the Philippines as well as in some parts of Europe, Southeast Asia, the United States of America, Canada and the Middle East.

The Lord has blessed their union with three chidren - Eunice, Jonathan and Ruth.

Foundational and Inspirational Books
by Dr. Dante & Cynthia Veluz

A comprehensive biblical study on the prophetic ministry for effective global outreach. 312 pages with illustrations and endorsements from Christians leaders.

A comprehensive biblical study on the apostolic ministry for effective global outreach. 504 pages with illustrations and endorsements from Christians leaders.

Lovelife Volume 1
A Manual for Singles and Engaged Couples. 140 pages with illustrations and endorsements from Christian leaders.

Lovelife Volume 2
A Manual for Married Couples & the Whole Family. 214 pages with illustrations and endorsements from Christian leaders.

Published and distributed by:

Jesus, the Heart of Missions Team, Inc.

An International Network of Christian Leaders & Workers Engaged in Revival & Missions (Affiliated with the Open Bible Faith Fellowship of Canada & Association of International Gospel Assemblies,USA-Phils)

PHILIPPINES
61 Cambridge Street
Cubao, Quezon City
1109 Philippines
Tels. (632) 438-1819 to 21
E-mail: jhmt@pacific.net.ph
Director: **Rev. Jerry Ambi**

USA
1140 Northwood Drive #225
Eagan, Minnesota 55121
United States of America
Tel. (651) 688-7311
E-mail: ochoace@yahoo.com
Director: **Engr. Carlito Ochoa**

CANADA
90 Church Street So.
Richmond Hill
Ontario, L4C 1W3 Canada
Tel. (905) 780-0916
E-mail: jescuadro@hotmail.com
Director: **Rev. Joven Escuadro**

JHMT OVERSEERS
(USA Headquarters)
Tel. (651) 688-7311

DR. DANTE & CYNTHIA VELUZ
Founders & International Directors
Jesus, the Heart of Missions Team (JHMT)
and Christian Leaders Summit 2002
E-mail : dantecynthia@hotmail.com

139